MW00582675

Torques: Drafts 58–76

RACHEL BLAU DUPLESSIS is an American poet-critic, whose on-going long poem project, begun in 1986, is collected here in *Torques: Drafts 58–76*, as well as in *Drafts 1–38, Toll* (Wesleyan U.P., 2001) and *Drafts 39–57, Pledge, with Draft unnnumbered: Précis* (Salt Publishing, 2004). DuPlessis was awarded a residency at Bellagio in 2007; she was the recipient of a Pew Fellowship for Artists and of the Roy Harvey Pearce/ Archive for New Poetry Prize, both in 2002. In 2006, two books of her innovative essays were published: *Blue Studios: Poetry and Its Cultural Work* on gender and poetics, along with reprinting of the groundbreaking *The Pink Guitar: Writing as Feminist Practice*, both from University of Alabama Press. Earlier work includes *Writing Beyond the Ending: Narrative Strategies of Twentieth-Century Women Writers* (1985) and *Genders, Races, and Religious Cultures in Modern American Poetry, 1908–1934*. (Cambridge University Press, 2001). She edited *The Selected Letters of George Oppen* (Duke: 1990).

Torques

DRAFTS 58–76

Rachel Blau DuPlessis

RACHEL BLAU DUPLESSIS

to Don with affectionate hopes

Rachel

SALT

CAMBRIDGE

PUBLISHED BY SALT PUBLISHING
PO Box 937, Great Wilbraham. Cambridge PDO CB21 5JX United Kingdom

All rights reserved

© Rachel Blau DuPlessis, 2007

The right of Rachel Blau DuPlessis to be identified as the
author of this work has been asserted by her in accordance
with Section 77 of the Copyright, Designs and Patents Act 1988.

This book is in copyright. Subject to statutory exception
and to provisions of relevant collective licensing agreements,
no reproduction of any part may take place without the written
permission of Salt Publishing.

first published 2007

Printed and bound in the United Kingdom by Lightning Source

Typeset in Swift 9.5/13

*This book is sold subject to the conditions that it shall not,
by way of trade or otherwise, be lent, re-sold, hired out,
or otherwise circulated without the publisher's prior consent
in any form of binding or cover other than that in which
it is published and without a similar condition including this
condition being imposed on the subsequent purchaser.*

ISBN 978 1 84471 334 9 paperback

Salt Publishing Ltd gratefully acknowledges
the financial assistance of Arts Council England

1 3 5 7 9 8 6 4 2

Contents

Acknowledgements

TORQUES: Drafts 58–76. Many of these poems were written during a leave in 2004-05; the Pew Fellowship for Artists, awarded in 2002, made this leave possible. I am exceedingly grateful to the Pew Foundation and to Temple University for offering me this sustained time in which to work. I also owe many thanks to the editors of the following journals for their collegiality and encouragement in publishing some of this work: *Chain, Chicago Review, Conjunctions* and *Conjunctions* on line <*http://www.conjunctions.com/wcidx.htm*>, *eco-poetics, Fascicle*, FUGACITY 05 <*http://www.nzepc.auckland.ac.nz/features/fugacity/duplessis.asp*>, *Hambone, Jacket* <*http://www.jacketmagazine.com*>, *Literary Review, /nor, The Poker*, and *Ur-Vox*. In addition I want to acknowledge the help of Shawn Ta of Temple University's Instructional Support for managing the visuals in "Draft 73: Vertigo." My warmest thanks to artist Liliane Lijn, who took time from her own important work to do a final version of the cover. Chris Hamilton-Emery and Jen Hamilton-Emery of Salt Publishing are to be thanked at length for their sustained interest in poetry and for Salt's list, of which I am proud to be part.

Grid of Drafts

Draft 58: In Situ

This was to be a beginning,
   a simple beginning, in situ,
      that is, in the middle, here.
An impossible task
   but tempting.
      Since all words dismember into invention.
For in (or by) the act of starting (staring, stating),
   something else takes shape.
   How
could It be otherwise?
   Shifts of it, makeshift, light shafts.
      Shadows fall, split.
Sequences of looming
   shimmer dark and dun.
   Whatever happens
casts fates in strange outcomes, hard to own.
   Two shadows blown
      is one way of hinting it.

This occurred, this was situated
   far outside the portal
      way before beginning,
harried and impotent living,
   dry rage, petals blown into the city room
      from flowering pear.
This was hunched well beyond the limen,
   not in the site,
      not in the room,
lying mangy, Ulysses' dog
   waiting for something:
      a promise, a claim.

This was to be a straight-line list,
   itemizing what was at stake
      knit and knot and gloam and glare.

Flowering pair? the familiar
    sway in the cool gray spring from
        whatever came before.
It was
    "begin anywhere":
        such fine and open-heart advice.
To take it
    slakes nothing, simply spins
        a word or sentence into void.

Without transition—
    no "then," or "so," no narrative,
        no "after that,"
a student jumped from a window
    of my workplace
        a few tense days before the newest war.
Broke sealed-up glass, a hammered brick
    to accomplish the act;
fell into it, propelled himself.
    Gravity
did the rest, it was only
    the 9th floor, dead and gloomy day
        blustered with cross-drafts and wind-chills,
no going back;
    shadows cast full sorts,
        wherein to fall.

One's building used as weapon
leaves a mark

one's stairwell
intimate dull concrete

one's city
broken apart,

high-pitched twist
of sirens, useless

work of a moment,
It leaves a shadow.

Hollywood militarism
makes some dead inconsequent

even unbloodied.
But it is not so.

A stunned crowd gathers,
nowhere to go.

A strip of yellow CAUTION tape
is caught like wool in a fence.

Suppose whenever I begin again, it's
        to back away from
                where this had been:
the simple questions on the edge
        why here, why this, why now, why him, and
                what is this?
What is this for (from) amid depredation?
        I just wanted simplicity, or relief,
                wanted to list items: a cloud, a dot,
a brick, a leak, a twig, a paper
        bone fix twisted in its socket,
        a fresh eye, a weed, the bugs, the pipe,
                and each thing gets a different torque: the brick—
that someone used to stalk and strike
        a leak they dig the street again to seek
                a twig—no buds or leaf pokes, may be dead

a hump of flower shrines and photographs
        down-melted wax beside the corrugated door
            a fresh eye inside clouded sights
a weed just growing randomly.
        These lines are little pikes of
            intensity, sticking up:
as from porcupines—translation
        "istrici"—or "poetry."
            Night: their waddling shadows
vector cross the road. Day: we pick up
        spines fell on the ochre ground,
            their souvenirs.

People march down the street
        with cell-phones busily,
            pilgrims in an ordinary pocket
that has changed, fraying, they are weeping
        vocabulary of loot and looting
            beads scatter down, and some are lost.
On impotence, rage, solemnity, paralysis
        to live this way, to have foreclosed like this
            (who jumped, was it he or I?)—
which is simply the time here,
        whose puckered patterns
            loop and wayward, snarl and twist.

So what motivates beginning?
        how face these shadows looming?
            "You" said you thought you knew
but then you could not say one single, little word.
        This block continued, too.
            A white paper on metaphor
"you" were invited to write
        and could not deliver
            in dream or in wake

a dim wake
　　　where the full moon sugared the roof
　　　a-seasonal
as if with snow or frost
　　　is what the dream voice
　　　　　said you have, or hove, to see, to hear
that genre of shadowy command from whence
　　　you sat up here as if in dream.
　　　　　As if!
Lost time
　　　fallen forward
　　　toward silvery globes
as if—as if! we reached thereby the far-flung glow of stars,
　　　became like them implacable,
　　　　　blazing, void, atoms pitched with number.
But still considering an azure flower
　　　(like fools maybe), as if single items mattered so,
　　　　　concentration upon one forget-me-not,
nomadic smallness in the workshop of abyss.

I have thought of worms, too.
　　　I have steppend my autre on worms
　　　　　(cardamom, basilico),
　without meaning to.
　　　Their shadows para-oidos
　　　　　mocking next to song,
and song beside itself,
　　　noman, nomad, nogirl, nogood
　　　　　just the sheer N of no,
gathers darkness inside shadow
　　　—it lists, it tilts—the it of all of this:
　　　　　How account for it; how call it to account?

DECEMBER 2002–JUNE 2003

Draft 59: Flash Back

1.

A half glass carafe,
a half-filled glass,
a choice red ochre chalk,
a felt-blue paper,
particular words for things
incite lines whose shadows
break in cryptic outlines.

The paper blue as sky, the chalk as red as ground.
These "vigorous scribbles"
do suggest "deep space."
Lighter feather touches
fluttering letter-farfalle
do recall long scrolls.
Calligraphy crossing depiction,
scrolls sometimes annotated
by their owners; on the side, look,
by that four-stroke egret,
a note by the reader,
as we might write something
in the margins of a book.

Depth, lust
and continuance
in glistening webs of letters,
learn their ethics from poesis
in orgies of fabrication.
Streaks, points, gleams, elation
articulate various desires,
and textures cry with pleasure
exacting the price of their plethora.

Such filiated evanescing "it" 's are there among
the apple gests we set to tempt the dead
       with the happiness of making,
       with the open bright of listening
       as if to larky twits of finch
       through light surround of air.
       Awe-full Emily
       dearest Sapph
       weirded trumps of Gert,
       alas, they cannot hear
       although we talk to them.
       We hold out a red box
       and walk toward them,
       the rainbow threads between
       unrolling and reknotting
       wanderful languages.

    Splay of cardinal-pointed questions make a rayed-out rose
    flooding the heart with alternative directions,
       the rose of desire inside the poem's patchouli
         and not ironically.

2.
How did desire get here? Hearby. By they-her or elles.
By elevation. A leg up. By He-and-she and birds,
by little one, big one, dog and good-bye dog,
baby-milk cup cracked and gone.
It was abrupt:
one death and then another
quick turns of the rope, like double Dutch.
And couldn't hobble-hop those fast-turned twists.
Got dazed.
And tripped.

3.
Was there enough kindling?
    Dream of packing a dead girl
    in a fold-over suitcase.
    And therefore Years were lost.

    Of covering women over
    with gigantic cloths, of snagging them in nets,
    was not a dream. More Years.

I zip my body bag, donate myself to science:
    "feminist." And secular to boot.
Wall-eyed between suitcase and body bag
I asked "are alterations possible?"
    A poufed-out plastic bag blows by,
    "Pathmark"® is what it says.
        This is an ambiguous answer
        whatever the question.

4.
Question:
Why use the alphabet to organize,
    and why not? Discuss.
    Suggest another mechanism of order.
    One form and then another.
Something that sort of ends, but sort of not.
    The alphabet is existentially funny.
    Lettristic vaudeville, a blood-orange horizon.
    Such obsidian wings
    on talking points sashaying zones.
    I mean there's satisfaction arriving at
    (English) "zed," and (American) "zee"
    but no insistence that anything particular be.

Other end points where "arrival" is dissolved?
    Maybe a grid with limits.
    Maybe lengths of ribbon simply
    cut to tie these presents.
    Maybe qwerty or another
    job-lot keyboard.
    Pessoa's was azerty.
    And there we are again—the alphabet.

But this is controversy
without particular point. One form or then another—
it means something, but in itself leads nowhere.
A Form itself, abstract thing, is not
self-evident in meaning.
It's not one Anything.
"Form" is its particularized clot,
its histories and extensions, its situated outreach,
its power and prods.
Who has designs on us? and Why?
What is the force of our conviction?
Something had gotten away from us:
urgency for justice, intensities of ire,
lime-green as the after-image
in the eye-teeth of unrhymable orange.

    Where is it?
    What are the real goals of this desire?

5.
My words get alphabetized, montaged in Flash.
The frozen gits and their long, sweet liberality,
like talking points, dance.
Not to oedipalized,
Duh to enterprise,
Me to non.

Could be Anyone's words,
Owed to Oz, or owed to Ez.
Splitting words into letters' high res
at the point of their affirmation
casting the pearly bits adrift.

How quick to fly they are.
Like cartoons, they're bonked and clunked
but always return. See, they return!

I put my words in flesh
they flash in shadow,
n-wards, pull and probe
thru fleece and flask.
Something propelled this urgency, this task.

My words are here among the layered pages
inside quickly moving time
intricate knobs with "wormholes"
breaking cross themselves and turning inside out.
Dark matter they seek,
sediments of unfinished business.
These layers slide across and enter
each to each as naked palimpsests.

A page: where every line stands up affright
porcupines that run ahead
in sudden light.

6.

                    Go
        words-away.

        Come-words,
                    Go wide, go way.
Not here, not here, not here.

I'm wanting
        to erase all words I ever wrote
        because they do not answer to what is.

And now
        how
        unbelievable was that?

7.
Since every word is three, there is multiplication
        that can not stop,
        can never be called finally to account,
        but is always accountable,
        can only be ridden like a wave and then another wave,
        folded in a thick green danger.

Since every word is four, there is concentration.
                    Blue light swells from earth
                    then black and there are stars
                    without lines and without stories,
                    no names, no myths;
                    just stark and starker far-ness.
                    Perhaps it is comforting
                    perhaps the rage of matter
                    overwhelms
                    but whatever else is there
                    we're
                    living out our atom-laden recklessness:
                    fruta da época.

8.
I wanted to know about making art and telling the truth.
　　Niente da vedere,
　　niente da nascondere.
And then the precise opposite
straining to see an other hidden side.
　　　It is the way the day is
　　　a yellow stain, a pool of pink
　　　is it autumn? or spring magnolia?
　　　The seasons fold
　　　and pile upon the bone and slash.
　　　The truth? It's true.
　　　Although I also laugh.

9.
Is it possible to say what might be found here?
Every decade another list of shadows.
I was holding this list in my hand
optimistically. But find I am deceived.
It is getting harder and harder to read.
My eyes? smudges of the writing?
a twist of the eyeball tightening into hard blur?
the magic marker streaked in the downpour?
Dry tears over blood-type headlines?

Listing and listening
—a great swath of names and citations
and the question what were they
what had happened
these suffering bodies
riddled and scarified, bandied, branded,
can the poem speak of it, of this
injustice, rage, despair
large amid the subjects

it must confront
at the bountries where it stands
to reckon
with, to
        recognize.

I was sentenced to this bounty-boundary task
because sentences came and then I made them
but did not make them come.
They are skeletons that move their bony oars
and pump through sky
pulling their way across the wakes
of mist-laden
mote-dridden air
        dedalean annunciations
        of our yearning and failure.
        Where is justice?
        How to get it?

10.
Along the cross-hatched backwash
        is a pileup of boats to purgatory;
        the dead are pulling the dead
        up out of the water.

11.
What co-insides with this?
vertigo.
gap.
where you leap (and where you land)
is the poem.
Being abandoned among detritus
in a plundered world.

I have lost a milky trail; I will never get it back,
but pick out well enough
red ocher marks randomized on turquoise skypaper.
Furia azul. And talk of this in reddened lines.
Enraged by our time. That simple.
That's what I flash on.

So, now, with no further adieu,
I stand here in absolute frustration.
"This is an orientation to the crashing parts of the world."

JUNE 2003, OCTOBER 2005

Draft 60: Rebus

The task is to see the riddle.
                    Martin Heidegger

A moonlight fall across the ground
makes the dark nouns brown.

Owl passing through this place
frightens the dark, a moment rent.

Quotidian = astonishment.
This wind arrives from outer space.

How to articulate fermented strangeness,
how tell the junctures charging us?

What syntax exposes these relations
these helixed twists of filament?

To juncture we are sentenced
inside a suppurating, blow-hard time.

It is the res, rebus conjugation
that offers *of* as pigment.

What visits us announcing where we are?
To say "angel" gets misunderstood.

But even a handkerchief, even
a spent bulb speak doubly

at once of loss and of ineffable
winged flashes of time.

Not possessions of possessives
but things requiring our Being,

equally breaking, slashed and torn.
Who speaks; who writes?

The dead. But they stay silent.
Who then moves words along

a little screen, blue-gray like sky?
C'était, ma soeur, la providence awry.

The living. Toggles of shame
and flame leech their veins.

Between these riddles,
Things present themselves like speech.

House bridge well tree
gate jug window tower

They say: it's so beautiful
couldn't you do better?

Or: you have made it; but then
you insisted on worship.

Thereupon
destroy.

Suddenly from this mattedness
in and out of nowhere in a fettered place

the *pure Too-Little*
swivels inside out

becomes an awe, *Too-Much.*
A plethora. Magnetic urgency.

Hinges of light, hallways, staircases turning,
spaces of being, force fields of ecstasy.

Now we feel surges of the overwhelming;
now we have a different angle on things.

Major dreams with guns. Must rescue children.
Everything I saw then was premonitory.

Everything goes wrong. Like a stone
a grey bread grows stale.

Can't cut it, can't soak it, unspeakably hard,
it's a twisted loaf we thought was fine;

it is the rock of our politics
looming on the table.

I wanted another desire, one bread after another
the green or greener guide of lune

I wanted a whirling list of hopes
hopes hopes hopes whole alphabets of H's

to evaporate and leave the sweet encrust,
a deep powder, a power inside the poetry

and inside the mind. I wanted—
it doesn't matter because

I could not get it easily or even
did not understand myself in this,

wanted a new kind of climax
at the center of day, the Of

specifying itself, as junted connection,
as counter-force, as transformation.

It seems as if I'm *not living*
on earth any more

at least the one I know.
The name of this place is—

Loss of Wishes?
Uncounted Dot? No-taste Fruit?

Headless Doll? Barbed Window?
Burning Book? Over-padded Chair?

Are these new Constellations
in our bell-vast sky?

Some They want to own the sky as
proof that They own us. Our Of is

our resistance. The poem offers
an exchange of rebuses, not a game.

This is not simply the world as such
but a world stained with other times

the riddle of rubble
that still speaks of

uncanny shame, of
alternatives that did not happen.

It's strange now that the Constellations
lie *upside down* as if tumbled from behind

turned into another hemisphere:
the W of Cassiopeia now an M,

and it stands for moaning and
muttering, for occluded humming

and for wolfish maps. Why such misery,
why such merciless management?

Klage, Klage. The disinherited.
Malarial muck for drinking water.

The twisted limbs of children
servitude, desolation.

I wanted to show you things,
the patient code

of things in a row to read—
rock, rope, doll, well, road

crystal glycerin rebus
of an empty snakeskin.

What will we show now?
To whom shall we show it?

If I were to cry out,
who would hear me?

JUNE–DECEMBER 2003

Draft 61: Pyx

> the enigma of the plural impasse
> Barrett Watten

where there is a "fatherland"
where there is "homeland"
one leaves for an "unknown land"

INTRO DUCE

Go with the old man,
tour his office, enter
each of the numerous ochre
rooms with artful carpet.

He tapped his cane, surrounded
by other men
showing the faculty or facility
a faculty for what?
Dogging his footsteps,
lone, loup, louche and
range-y,
still I was,
opposed.
Dunque I wrote not a word.

So then it was DAWN,
Dawn over the PMLA
bibliography

articles, books, festshriften
shrive me! father!

∾

Go, little lines,
singing in my sullen ear;
go, half-baked work
noting, and by the notes begin
a process of greeting.
Of gritting.
Without illusion.
Darkly, I listen.

BEG IN

"The melodic germ is marked 'icy' in the score."
What is the finding? is it loss or gain?

Smelling "the stench of stale oranges"
        gray-green spoil outlined in white
growing on their soft unpeeled bodies,
a touching quotidian
        a domestic sensitivity
amid influx of beetles,
        broken cloacas,
        and meeds of merde.
Was it hell rot or "he'll rot"?

                Secret words were present under
                the scintillations
                of concealment
                and when the page turned back
                an underneath came up.
                The hand shakes over the page,
                turning it, turning it.

[22]

IN-SO-MUCH AS

My mind stretched to the bursting point
with this enormity
with the continuity of the gun-sales

who live inside a slow rumbling pre-
apocalypse
incorporative clutter evidence
pilings, findings
phonemes of findings
selvages of findings
savage oscura clippings
the avant garden
inflame inflamed
inflaming images
and then moon afloat,
silvery eclipses cool down
in luminous cloud-shadow.
How to resist a world-system?
∿

Was there a before?
An inquiry before insinuation?
an interval before infamy?
an indication before interdiction?
Scumbling and "intaglio,"
inattention and incantation,
strict inflections inside blurred insinuations,
incandescent inundation:
Was this all of one piece?
And / or was it inconsequent?

∿

Perhaps it was like fireworks,
a scintillating power showered
from the sky.
The rocket explodes with a hit.
Colors emerge, splash space
with their mimesis of stars
red glare, blue flare
delightful disasters of light shooting up to them,
spraying sparks and glitter constellated,
round designs and extended arcs,
while everyone watching
diverted and entranced
goes ahhhhh,
for wonder.

IN RE

As for R, like a revenant, I wandered
far and wide
reversing, and revering
the streets and cemeteries
of the dead
and I saw the Monuments
to the Deported
stark inside me
as in a City
just at the tip
of my
circumscribed
Island.

~

The imagined sounds
shake your veins
with dirty rumbled tune;
the movement
        doubled cataclysmic dreams
bled over the four margins
of the round earth's
        imaginary consciousness.

        How to get a handle on it
        How to keep the rage complex

IN   CUSE

ledt hoo vill rhun de harmies,
        if I can gontroll th gredit

... thereupon ...

greasy flame of dead gas flare
        . . .
            a thick air
    and a stifled silence.

                uncanny
                cunning
                incarnate
                instrument
                prefiguring

                an echo chamber
                sinus out of schnozzle
                caught in the hiss

a birth of enigma
to which
one owes
and owns
one's own
enigma.

     ~

I had packed
I had saved
I had pretended
something else amid the dust.
But
there was no I, finally, and it
was neither here nor there.
The nowhere of in - - - - - - - -
prefixes all of this,
hinging, half-hung
half-off broken doors.

     ~

Mud swirls left from a flooded room,
       room bright, seemingly crystal, yet
deeply streaked,
a dream of death
      in which one feels one's own.

        Whole songs condensed
in single words
   whose letters sear the page.

The fingers split the pomegranate's crust.
Blood intensity
and seeds of ruby jewels fall out.

FAR FALLE

Say to the "lyrical diary"—lyrical! as if
this were innocence through which the burdens
of time might be redeemed—
        Say
that the Azure
        is Politically invested.

And then Write—so that words fail.
In order precisely that
they fail.

~

IN-AND-IN

Some narrow rat
hunting the ark
on Mt. Arrarat

The extra "r"
rises to speak,
to squeak
its little song
or songe
into the dear dead dark:

Bonjour messieurs/ dames
signori/ signore
Herrn/ Damen,
ladies etc.: Hallow.
It bows and twists.
Do you hear it?

See it? those
the peals
that queered its tries.

Look at the letter
just as it was sent,
posted in fact
during the Post-War.
What war?
You think you thought you know.
One in which you were born
or borne or bored
or bode
embodied.

Chasing this little r and others
into a concrete labyrinth
sealing them into the Them
that they were doomed to be . . . .

and never halting? never faltering?

~

In short, it was a day, and you are,
you stupid nothing r,
like others in this space,
somewhat on my mind,
being the little tiny Jew
poking a nose somewhere
to find something.

There is a rat behind the arras
he says. And may I cordially

introduce or interject or introject
that ratty little r—it's me.

A rat in arrears
scrabbling up Ararat
dragging its dogged bit of flesh
through all that—

IN VEIGH   IN   VEIGH.

How is it? I said: that the ghosts are so gathered?

Because they are palpable and present
buried wounds
the names that cannot rise and so they turn
and come as darkness thickened without sound

These Shadows make antiphonal claims

as words that fail.

ombra sono e ombra fui

Which are the words and which are the shadows?
there are no words, are only shadows
These spectra of tongues inside the very stones

and yet if one listens—there is no sound
in anything

it is the silence
of the "impetuous, impotent dead"
held back,

but sending letters, signs, signals, traces and
little gests
though one cannot read them very much.
It is too hard.

Facing an intersection
a knot of matted possible

the page a cavernous echo chamber
of that

—it lists, it tilts—The it of all of it
became a shadow
something dark and indistinct except
in edges, something
changing with the light,

but can be intuited and half articulated

in traces on the other side of inference.

IN STILL

Sovegna vos,

rem-Ember

and thereupon open

today's

newspaper

A rush of people across a bridge:
grift, happenstance, war, drought, need

mortal life washes us up on its shores
somber and singing
cracked hordes, cracked lips,
the quiver of sound, a planet
(under a sky dusted with lily pollen)
desiccated, decimated.
with what? empires? profiteering?
sheer misuse?

Not is as good a mark as *now*.
This shows the limits of the mark.
The harder meanings are social.

"For all intensive purposes"
"she's beckoning the question."

What is this the other side of?
What is this a margin of?
Forget "other."
Forget "marginal."
It is this very site.
It says "Sit down in it.
It's time now."
Now it's time.

JULY–SEPTEMBER 2003, JANUARY 2004

Draft 62: Gap

The 12 meter plug is now sealed
into its thick-walled shaft
inscribed with whatever words,
names and symbols
onlookers scratched
onto its lead sheath,
lead being that soft
like a pun on "led."

Sometimes it was graffito'd over in red.
Four styluses, available at the site,
had been taken up to write
stale, humble messages,
slogans, poignant bits, political signets,
devastating, simple, simplistic,
signatures, dates, and initials,
the usual signs of being here, words
inadequate by the conditions
under which and through which
we (they) are calibrated, in the nature
of this employment, and
in the nature of things.

After one part is covered with words
high enough so no one else can reach,
the stela ceremoniously (a rite)
gets lowered into the underdirt
prepared for it. This exposes a new blank
lead surface on which to write.
Greyland, gunmetal drypoint for tanglewords.
And people do. This goes on
until the stela stops.
The words have reached the top.
All in the ground, the slab

is capped with a plaque
like a dried out well or a played out mine.

Will we be implicated?
Listen.
"It is proper to go back to the shadows."

The lead is what it is; it cannot differ
from its properties.
And thus it did or will leech out.
Results are not explicitly predictable
but general parameters can be suggested.

Bitterness. Poison. Site damaged
into its half-life, quite the unconsoling term.
Dispersal along scrimshod ventricles
soak along faults and veins
cloaca inside fissure. This the shrine.
Like a "roof leak," like a "wall leak"
its origins are tricky to track.
The material seeks and turns,
it seeps and finds its way.
How not to be implicated?

What is the color and gleam of implication?
No one chrome or metal.
It is fine and unnamable in tone.
Dust of dimensions, beware,
red smudge, dried.

What is the shape of implication?
I cannot tell.
I know that it will touch your cells
is what I know.

Long as a line, quiet as most air.
Small as insomniac twisting.
Triangle fires, tangled rectangles.
Something disappeared once there.
Tell me when you know.

NOVEMBER 2002–JANUARY 2003

BEFORE THE U.S. INVASION OF IRAQ

Draft 63: Dialogue of self and soul

I don't know what to do
about this rampant hunger.
I've read Akhmatova
and live as if in vigil,
cold and stark, watching
the ramparts of my country
for some shift inside the walls.

> You say "as if" as if you sought a metaphor.
> Dark striated shadows flood the mind:
> It is All Rift. Crime awakens crime.
> Recoveries bargain and lose. The only rule:
> Abandoned in and by what Is.

In Swan, Denab pulses, implacable,
immeasurably more luminous than our sun.
Another strand of the unutterable
lump of knot, the shock
of *breathless starlit air.*
For if we took this fullness in—
something would change?

> Nothing would.
> Denab is too remote.
> And about others,
> as for their blood on the fruit,
> as for preventable pain,
> perversely too close.
> We lack imagination
> of the unimagined.

Yet "unimaginable" is Secret Twin.
I yearn to see the moon, to have clouds

break apart. Instead they close.
No metaphor. All flatness. No results.
This ran aground, cannot go on.
Is it possible to begin twice?
No, not sing. Just start.

> Then how will you select
> your emblematical initial
> for the first Word
> in that newly freshened book?
>
> Will it be poetic O of moon,
> the charismatic location
> for today,
> in suspension inside time,
> pre-colonized,
>
> one letter beyond N
> and completing the NO
> perfectly?
> Or perhaps the P of Paralysis?

Don't mock this; do not mock its desire.
It simply needs to be forgiven.
19 columns of impacted writing
are indexed under 26 letters.
Why zero in on one?
I'd hardly say that letters
do not matter, their brilliant serif-im as fire,
but thinking only of design, of mystical nets,
will not absorb the imprint of our time.
One begins already restless, enmeshed,
trapped, in fact, in endless twists.

It seems to me no gesture does enough.
The palette is plethora;
grief the news and rage.
The poem's magic eye
is startled by the page
where it should lie in peace.
Or so they say.

I never made that claim.
Tonight the planet earth, one total thing,
will cast a brownish stain
over our intimate, the big-faced moon.
Clouds are in the way.
And I'm resisting allegory.
Still, this is the moment of penumbra.

Here is the traditional theme
for the scholar-amateur
who contemplates a waterfall,
or anything, really,
that might be seen
as generating signs
for self-same self to read.

Sitting huddled on a city-deck
walking the plank of your life,
cold, even in May,
supposed to see an eclipse,
you barely catch a glimpse.

There is no Ought; just Is.
Trying then to read what Is
upon this murky path
scraped along a brilliant stone

a.k.a. our clay and iron clod,
magnetic mite that moves its milky blue
inside some arc—is fearsome.
Better to say "illiterate in these signs."
My eyes, my heart are stone.

> You say you want to see
> what you do not see. Or
> can't interpret whatever
> you do see. Pathos
> this motif. There is the said, the
> unsaid, the barely said, the next
> within the text, the fear.
> A page turns somewhere else.
> Vision's blocked at every turn.
> Accept it. This failure is the vision.

What's the covenant?
who is propitiated?
who assuaged? who profited?
The judge fell off his perch
and broke his neck.
He heard the news and lost his balance.
That was the end of valid judges.
Now we are led and judged by monsters.
Where is my place?

> There's nothing more for you
> than where you are.
> The saturation of
> stupefied unhappiness
> inside your stumbling heart.
> We're caught inside our time,
> a tunnel in a cave.
> No litter is neutral; no hope is uncorrupt.

Would cloud-caught moon
just reach that open patch of sky
so I can catch the eclipse?
The here and there do not match up,
the what I want and what I get.
10:28, 15 May 2003.

Such yearning to see
this little slice of time
darken preternaturally.

It looks to be going
into deeper umbra

What is darker; what is lighter
Will these clouds move?

Was this the hope, or that

Am I seeing it?
a smudged nuance
risen at the bottom of the moon?
The meniscus bubble of brown light
makes time visible in space

and a thousand miles of darkness
pulls like a dinghy
across the luminous surface.
Such strange stakes within the endless.

AUGUST–DECEMBER 2003

[39]

Draft 64: Forward Slash

The poem is the fosse
in which to cower
hunching down
by warehouses of power,

a sludge-filled ditch
where futurists once lay;
now backwashed debris,
now box store splay.

Turbines process
hot Things and then
distribute them, but nothing
is what you want.

Things no one sees
on always-on TVs. Not fake,
but not, as it happens, unprofitable.
Lemmings running on the take.

So my throat opened
like a snake's throat when it faces down
its natural food hiding in twigs.
And my eyes opened wider
swept by headlights,
fast drivers in fat cars.

But I could not strike, nor take in
all that I saw. I had poisoned nothing, hurt nothing
by myself, if ever there were such a thing
that had a choice apart from strings of stringent
stinging links that I
could barely bring myself to know,

standing uneven, aslant in the street
like the corner mutterer covered with a quilt,
bloated with poisonous fill,
although my electric other-selves
did damage where they found they could
all in my seely name.
Slash slash, it was too much; to be therefore
so close to overcome.

"I could not do one step at a time
or at least
I had to step
on many paths at once
with too few feet
to go around."

Content-Transfer-Encoding:
quoted-printable Blank Rachel,
I just wanted to let you know
right here by writing this, that
I too am a stranger in these tangled
corridors of strangeness
threaded through the buried graffiti and strata,
prussian blue over burnt umber
a glyph of the twentieth century.
So far, this one, too.

I limp the maze where other shivering walkers went,
the hurt the halt the broken.
I imp there, am a particular shadow
or third beside them, in a classical cadence
foregrounded by the habit of harkening
back to what we know, some idea that's so consoling.

But I am leaning, I am propped, I am fractured,
this is not walking but a shuffled drag.
I am trying to walk in the world as it is,
but all the weights and balances are off
sides, and listed, the whole range of scales
tilts, visionary ankle-twisted trail when I am
in this real world, pulling
a concrete plug or slug
my self,
whatever it was snapped
when I put one heavy-hearted foot
down on the concrete
one rancid day of mist or missed.

I surely need to learn to walk again
mindfully
where it is necessary to go.
There was ripped cloth and a hollow ring of bone
dissolved into a raining snow
of my own body falling slowly,
swirl and clumps
and I didn't want to know
     there was nothing I got that I had wanted yet,
     a little fuzz or droplet indicates its place.
     There was no solution to continuing to want

except continuing.
Wind rain of a shallow day.
Hot fix but the firewall is, as stated, temporary.
So far there is no fix lasting longer.
There is nothing more to say.

And so I haunt the spot I once was riding
under the road under the mall under the state
under everything, strata, engorged & fattening shelves.

Ghost. Yes, ghost. This one not complex.
Just the shadow isle of sunken hope and text.

DECEMBER 2003–MAY 2004

Draft 65: That

Foreword

Oku—farthest-within-dead-end place
no—possessive
hosomichi—path-narrow road.
"Back roads to far towns."
But the other translator
contested this, declaring his
"Narrow path to the interior" was best.

~

Road, water, mud rock weathered off,
portal in mist,
the fact of a long walk,
to see no telling what.
We were just going to talk.
Some lines, an errant sort, go here and there,
and that was it.

Dotted line around an air in space
there was once
someone there,
that
particular unquenchable
rounded genial and hurt
helpful worn humane

one;
and the space wherein he was
kept filling up with him
just the way one knows
in life
and so it goes.

But the water got down to a dangerous level
like the dark of photographs.

And now a dotted line, a moebius flash
one wakes and asks

what was that falls out
of range, what was that

event at edge of memory
left such a dotted line around a place.

Now you can come back, someone says,
a wish that cannot be fulfilled.

Now you can come back;
the joke is done. Trickster that.

It is not hiding; it is not a mistake.
It is simple, an unassimilable fact.

A moment: one sees "him" and
this must be accounted "ghost,"

another status, diffusing points
that even multiple lines and posts
cannot link.

A wave, a cryptic half
lip half-turned smile, an out-
line of.
He was given a bye
on the rest of his life;
he passed it by

with a wave
unwillingly, but there it was.

The stumbled byway,
split and split again.

The newly-dead try to say something. "Like poetry."
They have information. They know what they are feeling

but no words. There are no words
they say for it.

Something goes speechless, or it can't
fully explain itself,

it uses foreign phrases "comme çi, comme ça"
and "que sera, sera." It is debonair

like this, and not. It sickens and loses
slow and fast, it swells or sinks,

the body formers itself, as a former body.
Hands don't do the same or what they did

can't count on them and
breath, well, breath

goes slowly in the night, and here obstructions grow,
blackness lengthens and there are no

objects and nothing stands
in the way, in that one way

except carafe or crumpled sheet gleaming "normal!"
"Here!" Or in another tiny dawn,

that place: of its blankness,
of plenitude and unsortable impact.

Uprising is trying to invest words with alterest sdstated
altered states I mean

of meaning,
hopes and rages funnel into

one strange word. In Stranger change of scale.

That encapsulates narrative,

that uncanny opening layers everything.

Who knows about completeness?

That is a fragment. Like everything else.

JANUARY–MARCH 2004

Draft 66: Scroll

down and remember
little museums of the commonplace
incorporating clutter evidence—
forêt foreign dreams,
like a hut, structured
out of streaky layers of clouds.
"If this ain't yours, it's no one's"
trans-genic bacteria, plus us
need 4 more planet Earths
to all consume like U.S. citizens
So yell "Trigger Treat"
without fraying, or unraveling
Folded inside these intricacies
it's collateral wreckage
Is this the Tentieth Century?
Dream boy, glass tubes of water
hung on strings, all over limbs
where scrolls, where ropes unwound
in their own lithic labyrinths

to Resist Monoculture with
heritage temporalities
in which someone awaits
the uncanny
raffish as a basket
This is one more clot of rope
the lumpish, the odd, the lumpen
dumped together in a field
o sodden struggling Scribes
cannot keep up with this
You'd think tight knots would stay put
but this was not so, for
every letter made a slip knot,
and many serifs got used as Law.
Who is expendable?
"Every poem has an alter ego"
where throws of the die
do not abolish or resolve
fear, judgment, rage, and shame.

Scrawled inchoate specs
want a different outcome
want no extinct orioles
want to replace
Snide Rhetorics of "scare quotes"
from well-oiled power centers
After the first performance
people began to weep
twisted with pity
they had lived through it
while it happened to them
Again to recognize
they were the subject, subjected
they made few noises, all internal

Shame on every level
from cataclysmic dreams
whose color bled all over
this irremediable failure
coupage of mottled views
edge the guttered site
In mendicant contact zones
envoys, aureoles, reflectors set
by scratchy tain-holed mirrors
as if prescient—
It's their own abandonment, They had
epiphanies of mourning
with imprints of this time
evoking dots, blanks, lags, gaps

in vigil, vigilant
in doubt, double doubt
en route, rolling out
even perhaps to be forgotten,
deep in their own distance

whose intensity of conviction
signaled unfinished business
folded in a thick danger
Revenants smoldered
holding brands of sporadic memory.

That smudge on the wall
there at the abutment
part of the machine yet
when it wasn't, was
a dream of playing the harp!
a hasp? nothing could tune
the red and blue strings
colored tonalities of neon, framing
Mall & Interstate—
proceedings just 4.17% Homeric
shadows telling stories in
tanglophone poetry
Not a text and gloss but
structured as gloss next to gloss
no center, no side, just
swerving and looping
querying what aspect is marginal
how to travel it, how to rethink—

A nubbin-stub of charcoal
engineers an allusion to signs
no longer simple and
no longer complicit
but had no spot to locate
this desire for rough limpidity
that crystallized, criticizing
the gigantism of conventional beauty
"taken for granite," as against
a nekuia based on digression
pentatonic debacle,
at this fond du siècle.
So much wells up at once, thus
a lava-ribbon of text emerged
instabilities of liquid rock
with factures, overleafs and turns
to what; how ask why this is so:
one lives here, now in riddled
exposure—

And the Best-Loved Poems of America?

Stay with your luggage.

Patchy roads and fast foods
educational outlets in strip malls
pinguid gluts, unknowable nauseas
Shopping binge
Read the signs as you walk
read them, trying to figure how
branches suggest

Failed development paradigm
arousal to justice deferred
given box stores filled with stuff
Cheap as blood,
vigil memory error theater
plastics choking
both ruthless failure

the menace of marks
for "bored" viewers

Field guide to
the urgency
Photo op, then retouched
branded with the mark of this . . . –
Need Ur-freeze defrost
Need evocation of reality
the paper made of
considerable Post-Consumer Waste
and saying danger here and now.
The time emits a million tones

Not at ease here
can barely bear
to state the rage and grief but
can essay a letter, forwarding
parchment traditional for this act
in brightness, failure and vigil
versus a world-system
to stand and chant, roar and mutter–
with deepened meaning
how it splits the light into
colors under black letter,
phrases calling
maneuvering the underneath
a vast opening behind small letters
Barely. Anyone literate?
There are no sentences
performed without residue
Were some, were many,
half-hazardly used, destroyed.

and unspeakable, forgotten hopes
that alphabets nonetheless pleat and
gather.
Political autism and Rage
in tempore belli
with burning and dodging techniques
so where is our N to stand? No where?
need clarity of Letter, exfoliated
need possibility of analyzing
foregone recent history
palimpsested realism,
One sibyl-syllable, then another folds
tympanic membrane overloads.

Even with normal phonemes
forming dark words, they hardly suffice
for a smallest local hope; still,
arousal rolled back on itself,
making a scroll, another scroll,
constructing vectored shadow verses
tracing and sounding–letters
A coral yad, a mini-hand points
at Text. This insistence is fractal in
dazed & folded readings, for it finds
normal life a little odd but
out in full force,
unpredictably; and because of that,
hope started again and then again.
Calibrate the costs of this arousal
There are so many sentences
yet all completely haunted
such squandered squadrons
These "materials have memory."

Cry your hard out
But something else is needed.
Those dashing dots stare at
The Now: sublime recognition
the pain of thinking beyond
our air rights
inside a hundred and eight anguishes

Pocked and precious
incomplete bits and scraps
each word, declarative, going

perfectly en route, like spectra
extending to exilic plenitude
down along the gleaming tracks
that can transpose a suppurating
time to
"dimensions that are tightly curled"

in "the folded fabric of" this history—

Question "what now?"
may not assuage our damage; the
Here, the administered Interdiction

Forlorn shoppers
Cross-eyed interface of Not and Yet
whatever else we wanted from
quotidian detail and
plethoras; we need—
dizzy from a dream concussion
where 9/10 of the text lies buried in
dust—
to find these strips of scrip (tore)
that list so many tasks. To start
Again. Not again! In the imperfect
moment
again to unroll the scroll
like this. In Yet and Yes. *Id est*:
all the letters, N and Y, J and A,
X, and explore intricacy along the
way
e.g. inside necessity, where
something
sought transformative connection;
yet the
half-bleak, and half-pending
Tainted Spot still dominates
with its official, absolutist sign—

"Warning: No Person To Go Beyond This Point."

Yet need to seize that space to claim an exodus.

MARCH–DECEMBER 2004, JANUARY–JUNE 2005

Draft 67: Spirit Ditties

> Pipe to the spirit ditties of no tone
> John Keats, "Ode on a Grecian Urn"

1. The whole archive is an argument.

Is it with loss? Loss.
Is it with time? Time.
Is it with Legend?

Desire is the Tree of Legend,
distribution its Fruit—
all those tales
whose helpers speak in song
of feathers under oceans
of golden keys in caves
and of their recovery
carefully unlocked
inside secret doors
to unlock more
receding secret doors—

where did they get
these helpful "extra facts"
to teach those trapped inside the story?
There must be tales and facts
or maybe things in songs
beyond any story.

2. One lives utopia in weedy places,
seedy places, needy places,
weepy tail lights
red on drizzling road.

Lives uptopia in downscale spaces,
ripped-off acres,
impotent rages
locked in mazes.

When the weather seemed to clear
I went a-picking corn.
The backstory for this act
was "social surrealism."

I bent down
at the knife edge of the page,
cut every kernel from the cob
and re-sowed them in these misty furrows.

Faro, flaxseed,
oats and lentils,
silver corn and folly.
"Sometimes I add crayon."

      3. Bite and bark
      trunk and leaf
      rune and turn
      "I'm going away."
      Circle "segway" misspell morph
      wandering chorus
      wandering rocks
      melancholy matches
      its ink to the page.

      Bite and bark
      cuk and oo
      plangent and alone
      trunk and leaf

"Then I'm going to come back."
Sieve net
for fits and catches
swoops through scintillating air.
This is the ditty zone.

Rock and hark
fort and da
Dust in a pile, all swept up.
Jump and skip and skip and hop.
Snarky starlings
stalk the pocky park.
"Here I am, now I'm back!"
Crickets in the cool stone room
court the chirping laptop.

4. To travel to a father further
To start a mother-motor right
pillow songs on worn-down linen
and unravel every possible night.

"This wallpaper is Too Busy!"
hear telephone's behest.
"Don't you think one simple
understandable pattern would be Best?"

"A few years back, I had a frozen should."
That typo said what it could say.
"After all, you're getting older.
How can you live this way?"

Person a pinhole through which
this death pound, opened, roars.
Use a helper dog to fetch,
cold wet nose and scratch hard paws.

And look here at my hands.
They're both stained blue with gashes
simply (simply!) from sifting a few
woad-saturate ashes.

5. "I am my mother's joy.
She swings me round and round.
I don't (yet) know why.
Nor know 'I'."

6. House, and side house, other house
tenth house, darkened house,
memory house, house to the n-th

mix of babies children
mothers and dogs
waving at the train

encumbrance and small
things saved up, chipped cup,
bureau doily with a spot,

I think she died
I think he died
but possibly not.

There are special baskets
to carry back the reeds and rushes
used for making other baskets.

Little houses, little baskets
bark and strips, woven tightly,
impenetrable and portable.

7. Upon a time, this is a fact

one total page was inked all black,

this for a funny flubbering book.

At that same time one string of light

dropped plumb down

from sky to ground

in the gigantic intimate night.

Anamnesis, anamnesis!

Catachresis, catachresis!

That's it. Sez who?

Couldn't be. It's true!

Come and take a look.

8. "If you eat the food of the dead

you're dead.

If you eat just a bit

you're right on the edge,"

she said.

9. Who rising, stepped out over air eyes

lived in rubato, delay, slowness, suspension,

slow motion, picking crystal fibers out

from the background of her handmade paper.

The dead and time are birds
ticking chirping squabbling hooting
not here, not here, not here.
Cotton's named "the vegetable lamb."

Plus there is no time. The watch is broken.

But now the Door to the river is open.

You may draw water.

You may draw it from this very page.

10. Ye gods and little fishes

chow down on the kasha knishes

Smallest causes lead to kisses

Little Lamb God blesses blisses.

11. Doggie must pee
rub soft noses
tee hee hee.

Doggie must poop
flap soft ear fur
yip yoke yoop.

Dog must pee
and dog must poop
and dog must eat her doggie soup
just like you, my baby mine, and me.

12. I am writing about a bird who is a stone

but whorled and feathered. I am dedicated

to dazed noise enveloping its stubborn noise,

adding random poem dapple

to what the bird can do in song.

The bird can go gee-ee-ip

chakakakaka and churr, tcharr, chairr

zi-CHEH zi-CHEH and gee-yip-ee.

It sits alone, narrow and yeasty

singular and leafy

like a stone charm in a bread wreath

like a small stone in a fog wraith.

13. At the party, daughters
remembered last words
of their various mottled mothers.
"When will you ever
take my grand-daughter
to get her hair styled?"

And "Why don't you have
some highlights
put in your hair.
You'd look so much
better."

They remembered
these final words
forever.

"Have" and "take" and "put,"
"Have" and "get" and "look"
are anagrams
for female "ever."

14. Daughter with the baby mother
doll clothes on the baby's finger
Grander-mother feeding Knots
Someone not wearing any undies
Ooh ooh they all jumped about
They had the very blank tushies
of Very Bad Dolls.
I get someone to eat
who didn't want to
and someone licked the spoon I held.
Food was how they recognized me
like a storm brewing.
The suffering dead and the baby-born
learn to yield to the tablespoon.

15. Hey, you're fraternizing
with your father whose eye you scratched.
He has mental operations for the
very first time, he insists

puzzling out solemn lunacy
from his ceiling, did give him a heroic
medical lunge at story;
saving savior, he was imminent.

Did not stop talking then or when,
but kept on fantasizing all he did,
holding forth quite eloquently, in
astonished modes of moribund Id.

16. Dirty sheep by me are shorn,
they learn to lie up-end.
I piled up their stinking hair;
then I began.
Product got washed, beaten, oiled,
combed, carded, spun,
product twisted, dyed,
spooled, warped, woven, sized.
It was washed and fulled,
stretched and teazled,
then the weave was shorn again.

That whole family was
dyed in the wool,
a deeper, darker dye whose
pattern could not be annulled.

And the newly naked sheep
nosed around their field
herded by a hairy *pastore*
in slattern sheepskin pelt.
Someone had taught that shepherd
how to sing, o la-dee loo,
plus to praise
all pertinent muses
up top and back of work.

This total techne—
the hungry muzzles,
the dingleberry heinies,
the loopy wool,
the hand dealt,
the game as played,
the dye and snarl and twists—
what an unbelievable spectacle!

17. "You can't drive the car.
You're dead."
That's what Someone said.
But he certainly ignored that.

Dead, he got in the driver's seat,
and dead he took the wheel,
and dead as dead he tooled along.
Is this some joke? No. It's for real.

This buddy trip inhibits me
but my syntax sets me free.
"We took a wrong urn somewhere."
So—his funeral: it's your funeral.

18. She is hunched in the archway
plates of spoiling food;
she is living in the kitchen
amid old crumbs and scraps.

Living only when you're born
dying only to get dead
sound parallel, sound correct.
There is, however, a lot of slippage.
Hey nonny nonny.

She smelled bad as I held her.
The sudden entrance of father-ghost
in his hanging bathrobe
broke the embrace
with mother-ghost,
just as in that theory.

But did she need food
did she need anything?
I would go and get it, bring it here.
If she would tell me
where she was.
Where was she?
Or he. Plus he.
Then there was me.
Where did, or should I go?

19. hello, no
One who is the end
of me

No—
one who,

a no one who
at end
replaces "ME"
in the ditty-empty dhoti
exile of one
into the Other
via 23 points of quirkiness

with a whole
and a hole
and an X
and a hex, and a wordling text

and a blank and a hank and
a skin-bare shank
and a no no no

and no one knows
wherever this goes
from hand to hand
or lamb to jamb
where that No One
is, or was, and where the one-two
punch will land.

20. Pedal the bicycle
down the waterfall
while you suffer
"abuse from the bridge"
and "abuse from the wagon"
with crystals sticking out your ears.
This is one hell
of a cult de sac.
But it's impossible to turn back.
You keep on asking
"Is it day or night?"
The answer is:
"It's bushes."

We are in this phase, now.

21. The reason
I opened the book backward
is wanting to cross
the divide of time.

During the vigorous ransacking of cemeteries
the dead begin to speak.
The talkie-talk sizzles around
spliced, ticking, godless.

Agitated language clots
tie the living into knots.
Unstrung language sounds
smash the dog-gates of this Death Pound.

So I don't care what you've found!
Bind the dead down, derry down
and hurl all their excellent advice
deep into the ground!

22. Far-away distances, thick cold.
Stars twinkle, twinkle at other stars.
Planets move in oval swerves.
We don't know what they see or are.
But "Images say, 'Behold!'"

23. Limp laved leaves with wet late snow
crisp leaves hardening in full sum-sun.
The house of the soul
is filled with little things.
I am dissolved within
these tingling gleams
and the wild randomness of dreams.
The sight of a double river
is like looking in a mirror
at Rachel of the *longue durée*
with her five kinds of vibrato.

Beginning to lose things?
        Yo! you Ghostly feathered plot signs
and Hidden Gists to let emerge on
        marge of dawn songs'
porous Score—
        Songsies, give us just one more!

Although it doesn't sound as if they would
all these libations also include apple.

JANUARY 2005

Draft 68: Threshold

This what you wanted
    When you said you wanted "more"?
This being the other side of amusement.
    Damage. "Boiling gurge of pulse."
Listen. You have stumbled across terrain and
    Still could not escape this twisted langdscape.
What words? Eroded, choked, and stun.
██████████████████████████████

You wanted to torque. But you ended up here.
    Impotent rages locked in these mazes.
The page is slowly turning black
    ██ words ████████ ██ .

    ██ Trapped ████ interdiction.
        as if estranged.
Drained, ██ thinking impacted;
██████

Despoiled news piles ██
        paper.
The room ██ the doorway
        smaller.
██ leverage ██ this?   *Language is*
    Truculent syntax ██ threshold.   *a site of history.*
Analytic rages every day   *As the war returns;*
    ██████ lesions.   *its syntax recurs.*

██ I was powerless.
    ██ loser and/or ██ neutralized.
The loss systematic. Systemic.
    ██ happenstance ██
The helixed ██ , Plunderers and Bandits,
    Devastation and gloat,

Chained me █████ fury.
　　Blowup
　　　　　rancid

Impotence. ████████
What would constitute
　Political fulfillment?

A regime of predation.
Glut and revulsion
truckle the body,
twist discourse.

Will never return, ██ dreams
　　██ floating downstream ████ coral-colored cities.
Now dreams of human shit in doorways,
　　Lumps, humped-over ████
　　　damage
　　　　　everything? ████████
　　　　　　　What creased map? but never mind
　　That all roads　　　　　　never
Mind the sleeplessness, the
　　　　　　what action
Can

Who watched the outcome,
stalled stark
shades in shadow.
passive verbs.

Make somber portage ████████

Stacked roads had all but
　　obliterated
　　　　　no longer █ stay
　　　　static places,
　██ enter and　　the
　　██ interlocking

Whirlpool in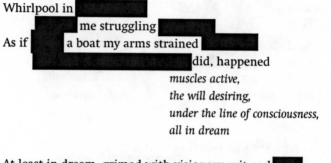
        me struggling
As if   a boat my arms strained
                did, happened
                muscles active,
                the will desiring,
                under the line of consciousness,
                all in dream

At least in dream, grimed with visionary grit and
    Muddy immersion, heavy going   *O dirty light of poetry*
Saturated   *shining on*
         underneath.   *a dream of transformation*
To get anywhere, to resist complicity,

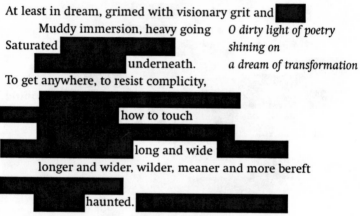

        how to touch

        long and wide
longer and wider, wilder, meaner and more bereft

        haunted.

      Historical tragedy? This is how it feels.
        Such sorrow obliterates statement.
             "No words for this, and these are them."

But it

emerge

along the mud-crust edge.
An

plausible now—
Is it to flood

threshold.
Plunge haunted water.

JULY–NOVEMBER 2004; APRIL–JUNE 2005

Draft 69: Sentences

Impossible to write a poem.
No sentences can be made.
Sound founders, kitschy gabble.
No collection mechanisms seem engaged
except razoring facts from the newspaper page
to which I am sentenced.
                Writ cannot be served
                by these statements.
                But writ is served on me.
                I am put on notice, a fleck, a stat.
                And this is it. Words are suspicion,
                Syntax is contamination, structure pat.
                Praise praises itself, blind and unctuous.
        Language corrupted, corrupting,
corruptible.

So let's be going, here and there (way away)
(you and I) (hand in hand) (obviousness and flatness)
(pattern and practice) where the sum-set disintegrates into crumbs
that street birds squabble over.
There is no revolution via cleverness. Just try to leave, it goes
da capo al niente
over and over again.
A loop, a crack; a loop, a record crack
a loop, a crack in ricochet and stumble
no end sonority, just middle muddle
trapped inside repeats, inside taunts and taints.
The point of these statements is crude.
                But accurate. And deeply felt.

              I am sentenced to run
                    a double track
                        propelled or pushed in one direction once
            compelled or rushed down others twice,
                        this semblance of motion

returns "I" to a near-same spot.
Then "me" freezes, breathing
manipulated air in winded rasps.
And it isn't as if this "I" has gotten nowhere,
is it?

Now what?
Each <the the the>
its politics of deceit
each <is is is>
every one a crash,
skid, overturn and strew across the highway
plenty of gaper delay
"it's ok, it's not me"—
illusions any watcher is exempt.

Stare/ *Stare.*
Eng. or It.
What words are there to quarry?
To look at hard and much
To be as such
All words laid out, laid down seem to *be*
words. War words.
Buy words. Even my words. Still and yet
I'm sentenced to no words.

How fake was that?
Don't these words count?

How would they count?
I have no press pass. No credentials. Not embedded.
This stands at the margin of edge

without particular brands of "I"
to greet you with.
Only you alone are listening,
perhaps; and thanks.
Or maybe not, can't count on that.
This is the onset, an embittered cramp.
This is the symptom.
Some books so hungry.
Some people so angry.
They could be called insatiable.
Sentenced to this.

Perhaps there are too many sentences.
Yet all be completely haunted.
Mouthpieces for gravel become
themselves stone. The sentient
pebbles left on graves are hapless
markers of my in-strangement.

Impossible to write
       if there is a "radical-putting-to-question"
       of art,   which there must be

       if there is any "putting-to-question" of
       reality,   which there must be

"Where we live and what" is the rest of that
       formerly noble statement?
       slogan of the brave, it shrank

       Dream of dignitaries
and megabucks.
Rip the books.

Why rip the books?
The book, the books contain our hopes.
To rip them
is to concede
to grope.

Luminous distaste.
Don't make me laugh!
So what? So you are being jerked around
and knotted; so you are roped
and pulled aground.
This is news?
Well, it stays news.
Their masterful escapades
and plundering moves
and thuggish scaffolding
become "your life."
The title was written with a knife.
The trick is, Watch It.
The trick is, Watch Out.

It Is
impossible not to write.   Not to; Or to.
Double judgments frozen within
            paralysis, which neutralizes its own stasis
                    into even further stasis. Into minoritized acts.
                    Sentenced to reject the sentence.
I am looking for the court of appeals
        for the court of residue
        for the court of last resort
        for the court of standing.

                Ghost poem, ghost poem
                poem on the other side of the poem

wraith poem, wroth poem
        poem of inadequate sentences,
of voiceless vowels of uh uh uh
stuttering
schwa-wards, grunting,

         and oh
if the lyric impulse strikes,
as is its wont, a poem of unique luminosity
and loops of beautiful o.

There is hardly any place to stand. I won't say "no
    place" because of boredom with melodrama.
But cannot write one word except
      the ones that say I can't.

Or two for saying <it it it> atilt the listing site
and <that that that> upthrust through the business section.
    Plus <the> and <is>.
    Four words hoarse
    as caws of crows
the eh-eh-eh-eh and then the ah and ah
tally-counting over every corpse.

      Is this what residue remains?
      Could the Sentence be suspended?
Could the Poem come forth?
      Or is it simply unnecessary,
flat out.
    Debating opinions does not matter.
    The whole is more intense.
"The letter has fallen out of the book of laws."
    Acknowledge this. Face it.

And then, and only then
will Shadows shudder
        shape wobbling alphabet outlines
in and out of nowhere in a fettered place.
Which constitute a register of loss
        that must be claimed
and mourned
        from here to there
        from it to is
        from the to that.
From such letter bits and snags
        what are the words?
                Who will set them out?

Flies are little people with wings.
They're me; I rub my thready hands along large things.
I taste the germs sucked through my hollow mouth
the sights that clarify my crystal-facet eye.
I look around me
waste pretense all the way.
There is so much never to say
filled with gists and drifts.
There was never so much to say

in this tensing buzz of poetry.

A lot of words to say there are no words, just rifts.

What is "the behest of this reality"?

Possible, word by letter, letter by word,

trying to true, again to enter and

engage the saturated task.

But this poem has to exit.

This is enough to mourn.

Impossible to stand it.

JANUARY 2005

Draft LXX: Lexicon

A
small piece of Apple; how agreeable!
          as something Anyone could accomplish.
                    Cut an Apple.
Make eight slices.
Anyone might want to.

          And accidentally
          might array anything,

          i.e.: Address Abyss.

Blasted Bloodwing, fast-flying bitterball,
bright birdish bleat
          it makes, when Blown to the side,
                    its beautiful tree bulldozed.

 It and we live, Bested by and
          bound to particular plunderers and Bandits.

Was it Clearly
choicelessness? or complete inattention?
          could it be collusion? However it happened,
          a catalog of conglomerate Collisions

demands this drawing, this Drafting.

These draughts doubled the dark,
          like drawing water from a well,
                    a will. A wall.
Its dowry was
          diasporic debris,
                    but out of this,
          distinctive desires

          emerged.

Every mark Electrifies the shock
every Erasure encoding each desire's eye
every Entrance extorts its price,
                         every Escarp
          exposes the danger of falling

                    and after the event,
                              after errancy,
the fall
          extends enormous waves; its echoes are

flung, F
          lung out, flooded. This any fool fleck
flickers as it flails forward
          its flat foot glances
          further down and far,

for it finds

green a-gleaming!
          Grass Writing!
          Is this mirage? The greedy subject Gasps,

                    Gorged by, gouged by need.

How any thing ever holds together
          homing to the pinhole!
Held by what?
          sight of that home, or hone, shimmering
among bristled haulm of

the Irretrievable; the Inchoate; the Impenetrable
          Is—? Is it.
          Incited thus

into Incipit, will Investigate such
(injurious)
(ingenious)

junctures, as the
J's of "jour" and "journey."
 Patterns of gap and joy, striped, jagged and athwart
 joined, like

a knitting, perhaps. Perhaps just like a knot
 snarled, tangled

yet lofting, lifting, a clot of balled-up dust,
its little lurch at the limen, blown by blast or loss.

 "Looks like you're writing a letter; are you?"

 "Lines lurk in Letters' Lucky Lenses,"

in order to Measure this matter, these bits of Matter
in order to Measure the mourn, the morn and bourn,
she and it and somber middle Marks,

noting
phonemes
like No, and
 nothing; all plus nothing.

Nine the muses, named the Nomad,
nine times N and ten again.

 "Will no one tell me what she sings?"

O
Oddly desperate question!
        only of This: all
orts of remembering-forgetting. The odd, or
        the odds approach obliquely
over the bridge, folded in an Orphic cloak of
        Or: a white field sprinkled with opaque dots
from which emerges

One snake at a time.

Poetry/ schmoetry.
That's it.
        That combination of panic and skill
                you see before you now.

And it was a question.
Queries about purposes and outcomes.
        Dazed quagmire. All these
are really quixotic qualms
                given one is in deep, deep as
                can be.

Deep into Ribbons, yet
roped with Randomness,
deep in reciprocities of damage,
        deep into Resistance
        whose Rengas
repeatedly linked by loops between
        reach the road down which to roll.
Unroll.
        Recall.

Speaking shadows are always shocking.

Through solid sheets of silver sky
Wispy song clouds slowly slide.

The strabismic lens of any shard,
as she said,
stops me dead.

Stark
startled
stunned:
serial synonyms.
Thus, to satisfy one simple qualm,
should make a smallish summary

of some of the *the*—so

      Try the tidy part: that 'twas a tender-tinder thing
   all tinged with texture.

Unsolved and unresolved,
   this crude and rufous surface
   shot through with Uneven velocities of signs
   urges

Uriosity.
Urrealism.
   The Ur of all this
   Passes between us.

From void to word, these cursive vectors dilate vision.

For words wished to wander interior wasteplaces, they
wanted to weave and weigh,
to work through all this without weakening.

Hence their x-axis will be syntax

whilst their y- is why:
why here, why this, why now, why me, and what

      is this?

Trapezoid letter pileups sharpen like razors.
      Zoom in on the Zohar butterfly.
      Zoom in, abecedarian,

for authorship is always displaced,
              to words, to letters or to angles,
                      in a space ambient with amazement.
      The whole archive becomes an argument.

Blockage, for instance, brought up from the background,

conjugates the crisis with clay verbs and citizenly pronouns.
      Consider cinders, consider the badger,
consider
complete

Defiance.

An edge exacting, exacted, exceeding
      even Events.

Finish
      with these Fractal fragments firm.
      Though first and foremost
          they flicker in the fosse
          unfaceable, unforgiving
          as fact.

Go forth. Gauche forays into the underglot
     will gather the gift.

What is the method? Generative.

And generally dazed.
          From all that gleaning.
Gleaming.

Hard to tell which hungers hinge to home.

In any event,
I woke inside it, in intricacy,
               and immediately insisted
                         it
                       was
                  "impossible."
Industrial Grade Server Needed.

Nonetheless was Joined and enjoined junctures,
          watched those juiced-up A's and J's
                    angels and jacobs
                       jousting.

          Was them, really.

     Could not in fact refuse.
          It was a call or command,
          and I got knocked down into the deep keep where
          command was keystone.
          Held down, under the knives.

But luckily, released.
This time, in time.

Clunked the Lintel, clipped the Limen.
            Limped and loped.
        Each smudge, each midge
                each sanctified allotted dot
loomed like a ledge.

Momentos of method, margins on the march
            moved beyond my wildest management.

Notes, in the night, energetic, nicked normalcy,
yet this *was* the normal, entering almost beneath notice
            near,
            here
            where
type O blood dotted on the page.
Of openings, Over and over, and of older hope.

            Strong optic, maybe the
            only one.

Project the Project.
Pile and repile it.
Up Periscope in pinhole.
            This pulsing present
                    cowers
watching current performance of Powers—
            This place, this place, this place. Poor planet I pray,

perhaps preaching

quote unquote
only to the quire

but Ready to be ready.
Reaching, wretched, returning
        to roam the groundwork of resistance.

Small sparkles sprinkle the strata.
        Apparently inconsequent Strings of shims
        shatter. Matter.
Space a sketch for struggle
        seeded/siphoned/shaped
                        by other skeins of other spaces.
What triumph?

Torn by the tripwire;
trapped.
        Are these trees here
more sacred trees
        than any other trees?

        Undertow or undertone—sound undefined.

        Rubble Unread
        underworlds Useless—
        the Uncanny urgent

will anything teach us?

Vast octaves vibrate the Wunderblock;
        vulnerable voice of the Void
visionary
with a volatile conviction

wafts up to us. What will it say?
                Words wash down the watershed, aswirl.
wandering chorus
of wandering rocks

We are watched and watching.

Double-axle reflux,
    Praxis indexed under every letter,
    and letters, excited, extend themselves
    copied on the
    ® trademark X—x.

    Y and N and R and X.

Your "blueness," your "silk,"
your No and Yes, your
Yes and No, yoked.
NegativitY. NecessitY.
The letters are yeast
kneaded into an unregenerate bread.

To blaze through the frozen zone
        filling zeroes with colors.
Zee and Zed. What is to be said?

And Here come allegories of anything again,
    a-leap
amid alembic excessiveness,
    alert as can be.

        These Are the Alphabets, claiming,
            disclaiming,
            declaring
            Attention.

Here Bundle button bead book and bone.
    Trobar blues
        and buzz of Bozze.

Here Collect the crumpled scraps
of confusion and calculation.

Dailiness darts here and there
in ditches of damage,
proud, distinguished
and obdurate as ever
before disappearing.

To express this entanglement,
this evanescence
I entered the errand

fatedly.

Far-flung familiars
filled the fence with photos and flowers
to remember
to fold
to fight fell feelings
of foreclosure.

Grand gests got made by
Graffiti vertigo.

Horizons of light opened and hallways,
although homely, held
humming Hemispheres.

Inquire at the intersection
the fate of the instrument.

Justice.
Just that.

Know
      the shock of lack, the break of dark.

The fuggifuggi of lemmings,
      the lash of slash,
            the if of glyph.

      In the middle of the malice, of the malaise,
they mouthed "Macro-economic continuity"
and now you know, majorly, what that
Means.

Come,
      let's go N-wards.

      For other rewards.

      Nice,
      very nice

      but not enough response.
      No way you can exit; the news is here.

Opening
again the sheer
oddity of it,

the fact that these specks of matter exist
are sentient, and do each other such great harm,

and here we are
at close range.

Poesia pura,
poesia para
pushed together,
spliced precisely,
might (potrebbero) provide a parallel, pebbly path
     of primary perception
     and propulsive power,

though any poem's low-res pixel
     pretends to propose

only a queer, a quavering practice.

Of that I'm quite aware.

Quick rumpuses
of Quiddity
(essence? or quibble?)

rustle wrestling with all of this.
Register the
resources
of what is and what
could be:
the full reach
of rectification.
A recurrent restlessness
is trying to resolve,
really without ending,
resisting the regime of
rigid resolution.
Call this desire for
Reverberation.

Shadow of shadows
place of place
noise on the roadways
intensify the reasons.

Draft 71: Headlines, with Spoils

Night sky, wet roads; headlines thick,
    big-font lines, the whole shtick
        in I Ching throws.
Auto and plant emissions linked to fetal harm
    bling bling—"linked to"
        but, as stated, "no cause for alarm."

The great hinge allowed only small openings
    along irregular lines of split emanations
        whose glut-fonts roiled from dark to dark.

        When I threw this as far as I could,
I didn't understand
    that all I'd established was the size of the acreage
    and the smash of the throw
that now I see
    as ideogram debris.

Hungry? eat sugared salt.
    Covenant-less?
        It's you become suspect.

        "All of this has been reviewed and is legal.
"However, I am sorry" (as stated)
    "that there are perceptions
        "and allegations of ethical lapses."

Of spoils and spoilers,
of the rotted meat governing the ground,
    glyph for acer-rage;
        of the spoils of war,
            of "smash and grab" economies

and the spoils of invisible war—
    "Trick in the full
        tricked
      sense of the word."

"12 hours per day for a pittance, living
    "12 to a room, working
        "in fenced-in factory complexes,"
            nailed to the sewing,
            chained to fabrications.

            Who controls these junctures?
            who prices these conjunctions?
            who mines the evisceration?
            Another walks beside me, not an illusion.
            Revenant, tell me if you know
            what land am I? and you?

        Whether this you/me one be plump-full or denied,
        obese or starved, run down or over-passed,
        our acts spin little balls of dust
        from the lint stream of this air.

There is a garish palette of superabundance at an undisclosed location.
Shopping binge compensates for a low industrial sector
Buy enlarge.
Freedom of Choice! ("linked to," as stated, "no cause for alarm")
And then the prototype robot-soldier
"readied, aimed and fired at a Pepsi can,
performing the basic tasks of hunting and killing."

        So That:
        This work will never hit
        the post-production stage,
        because

        Tanker Sinks Off Spain, Threatening Eco-disaster

The ecology of everything holding, breaking, presenting, emerging, swarming forward into linked emergencies. What is the damage done? to whom? how long to cover over? How will the "R" (find and replace) ever recover? Watch those startling sticks of chance get cast, and yo, your name here.

> Begin anywhere,
> throw by throw.
> Out-there
> connected
> to the over-here,
> must talk of that.
> A Cruel Past Lingers
> At just this time of year
> the light changes.
> No leaves yet
> so the air shines.
> And grit flies everywhere,
> blows into the eye,
> that hurts and tears.

Being choosing articulating refusing detailing
along the seam.
To keep track of grievances means living in fury. Forget
recollection in tranquility. Try collection today. Any day will do.

> To search this otherwhere of here,
> do you claim instruction?
> This might be it.
> An eros of production meets the detritus of over-kill.

> "'Smart dust' is now in prototype," which means
> "communicating sensors, tiny grains of sand,
> "might be strewn by the thousands
> "on fields and forests, all over the land.

"Envision such sensors monitoring
"forests for fire, warning
"soldiers of dangerous substances on the battlefield,
    alerting
"border guards to activity in remote areas."

Who strews, who reaps?
What is it to be tracked? What catch
to it? what caught? what purpose to deploy?
What haunt imprinted? Who
at stake? Why
tracked? why fought?

Flakes of flinty info. fly
directly into my third eye;
I see my second self
hard pressed, dispersed
through far-encumbered fields,
watched by the monitors of dust
            swept in
            swept up
            swept out
            swept over.
The monitors go down.
And then the glass goes dark.

FEBRUARY–MAY 2005

Draft 72: Nanifesto

Insist on smallness.
Scale down clutter.
Critique monoculture.
Build of it, not on it.
Clamor alongside plethora.
Argue with archives.
Loop your vines between the trees.
Never forget the accidents, though they teach almost nothing.
Do not fail sadness.
Build tight baskets.
Explore the transverse torque.

Destroy the merely consumable.
Refuse to buy it!
Declare a program.
Begin beyond it.
Link the emergencies.
Examine the inexplicable.
Demand polyphony.
Live in empathy.
Cross the void as you imagine one particular atom does it,
wobbling and transgressive.
"Drink from your personal cow."

Saturate the imperfect moment with intransigent audacity.
Teach the law of unintended consequences.
Meditate air threads in angles of light.
Consider the mite, the mote, the mute.
Affirm the loosened whup, whup, whup of practice.
Sew and freshen, wipe and preoccupy.
Wash mirrors with white vinegar.
Seek dark matter.
Show conscious energy.
Persist in negative care.
And compare the properties of reeds.

Wake in poised glee and utter irascibility.
Respect honey, and even more, the bees.
Ject every jective.
Investigate wild asparagus, for it grows oddly.
Cry your heart out.
You are both tied and freed, therefore resist.
To smash the fourth wall does not change much.
Gather the residue; credit its vitality.
Foreshorten blab, but lengthen liberty.
Compost the clippings of Logos.
Step deep into your shuddering boat.

Work for reverberation.
Encourage the birds, perhaps by the homage of whistling.
"You must talk with two tongues."
You must also shuttle.
Demand accountability.
Display minority.
Encourage the mind-of-its-own.
Let it demand a second cello!
Card the tree-wool carefully, for we already live in the absolute,
in a passionate state, in a violent rage, in the now, thoroughly
impatient, this much comes clear at every bitter instant.

Scroll, and run after unrolling.
Work in anxious panic and implacable assurance.
Keep the rage complex.
Make somber portage over grounds of loss.
Stare down the guns. But still remember
"in war the one who aims the gun
is not the one who pulls the trigger."
Be brave. Stand equally on both legs.
Seek intransigently the smallest information.
Stop snoozing.
Credit your own complicity.

Acknowledge tiny jolts of motivating outrage.
Hike in strong boots to wherever a good *there* is.
Feather the interstitial room.
Dare compare the little with the large.
Slide the pipette into the wall
for refugees from the merely agreeable.
Convert no one. Do not seek to.
Plunge with any word under its surface.
Appreciate when things go swimmingly.
They converge even when they hardly join.
And let the handkerchief speak.

Produce, for the wobbling micro-tones, syntax and sedimentation.
Streak them with whatever happens.
Shed sidelights on the middle dawn in golden tree and through.
Refuse to design Futurist golf sweaters. Just don't do it.
Trip and stumble on the dot itself.
Take possession of its little space.
Express entanglement as you fall.
Engage in pentatonic insomnia.
Affirm complex responsibility.
Any platform. Any wort. The trace is exigent,
even if almost obliterated again and again.

MAY–JULY 2005

Draft 73: Vertigo

Prologue: Even Tie

Viva, fidgeting roses!
Do men interrupt them
vexing blank calyxes to prompt them?
Vote volta-face for diagnosis.

"Already with thee" vs.
alterity of thee—it's heady.
Are you Ready; are you composed?
Can you go a third vertiginous road?

Light comes thru the letter.
That's what one awaits.
An alphabetic knock "oe vert"
at the folded gates.

Sirenic joy! the site erupts—to pour
its cockamamie allure
on the fragrant cipher
exfoliating separate, e-quill plunder.

~

Summary? None.
    Implications?
        Impossible to tally.
Can only cast
    Arith-mantic letters
        on scintillate planes.

Given these odds,
    all bets are off.
        Not a joke.

Except it is.
    Bone on bone
                shatters One
Ossessional
    Os, dotted, indebted,
                doubled by being cubed.
CALCULATE: that
    oreille minus oeil
                é-gal le R.

Early morn, Blue I awoke,
    off-sides a wicked
                A Noir-teen,

"One coo, daddy.
    One coup beyond the die.

            Plea: enlist, instruct me,
                still a verge ensign.
                    Co-opt me, dado!"
Whammy!
    Beaded angel thick dark wing in-pli,
        aquiver,
        arrives to deliver
        osmotic hammerlock.

    Such angelic spectral "Men"
        as Ben, Lance, Dan, serve as Cum-
Stances all to tune elle, as knights to
defend her flotsam aphrasia,
her
        silk thirsts
            like voile de gaze
            like veil de gaz
            sheer mist layering thick mast.

This marker mixed with cool of day
gris-gris nimbus spray
altocumulus of disordered fate
was "recalculated at a different
        sampling rate."

What is the cause of déjà lu?
Is it lune in the day sky?
spume in the night sky?
Science cannot tell you.

        But other HYPOTHETICALS relay

           ringing dub-bells of the Page
           feather of the father, twisting down
           flume of the tant—so much, the such;
           all these twangs of tweak
           fake "little virile reason" hymning
           ardor at the ductile edge of perfect
           Hymen
    which is the knife edge of the page
    which is the gutter of the page
    which is the emptiness of the page.

Enfolded pages' pips of quire
alter protocol

is why.

This is scientia. This is info.

Plus, aren't you just
glad to see me (and I, you)?
Salutations—forward post.
No man no man no man made this ghost.

THE CREASE   NUMBERS   THE LIGHT
SEIZE IT,   CHIEF WRIT.   ILLUMINE. OR NOT.

Set sail!
        cries blank-ful circe knotting and unknotting tulle
        (salut, slippery hitch,
                        shortsplice,
                                sheet bend)
        wreathed sway lashed on hawser:
        Such charms and placards rolled in
            conjugated tarp, flag out!

                        No aura, no lore's enough.
            All elevation's ordinary.
        But Verse in Absentia
            sheer Number
            the ur verve
                        Cues up her Plume.

NO ABULIA! HASARD
                        all the way.

Unfurl the sail, let's go.
     Tie me to the midden mast with fresh sirenic daft
          against the ocean's rushing surge.
The site pure recognition   (sing to me, I sing to me, to you)
     constructed from enormous loss
     whose saturated gaze

          stares

IN / FROM / BACK TO

VOID.

Voir-dire engulfed in songes of foundering.

Vertiginous torsion of the phantom judge.

To take the dark one in and not (and yes) be drowned!

danger
signs
sortie
ledge
from the rune nexi

high waves breaking on Il Capitán
and ghost fossils large as jellyfish imbedded in black stone.

hooked   wrack   ffloret   alt-   knotted

dawn   brine   quirk   chord

orthography   -eur   awl   document

lenticular   abyssal   gris   -ite

arc   wrecks   PROLIX   letter-knife

diasporic   gothick   shiva   TALMUD

tha   thee   this   —th   unrolls.

HAS ANYTHING HAPPENED?

WILL IT?

Contestation.

To have always taken place:

the blank/ the black   a blanker/
glossy blacker taste of Pantone ink.
Although

NOTHING IS EVER ENOUGH
even into extended telling, even unto toll,

each common number counts
       as (q.v.) penetration and/ or fellation of vanishing points,
       vigorous additives scribbling IS / IS NOT.

Each Factor goes astrew in gale force winds of Primes.
           Each pulls (as if!) across the wide, wild dict
           recto-verso, mercurial im – mage,
           counting onesy twirlsy three, infinity
COMME SI
slit with knife at the endge of folded page;
COME, SEE
what you have done.

Sybilline bones rattling
the gristle-knots of No Frage, the shipwreck, no question 'bout IT
         implausible chance
         improbably
            CAUGHT
                   in the flung net of starry night
                   as if it were this or that abyss
                   as if it were hilarity
       as if it were, oddly (even)

FINISHABLE

      scored like an OEUF, at ZERO

(no one wins this lottery)   (power ball bobbing on the ocean)
      watchful, doubtful, dizzy with
        scintillation, engulfing endlessness in itself: THE

stark

formless

letter

in a universe of outriggers. ADDS UP TO WHAT? a here dispersed
into stubbornness, WRITING as ceaseless act, a meltdown into any
molecule, the clamber of syllable, the chunk-stave ladder labyrinth
at the far, far side of Page, a letter 23 of 22 lurching out

beyond one single alphabet's constellation of entanglement.

IT IS

another other trace, or mark, or sign.

MARCH–APRIL 2005

Draft 74: Wanderer

Book I

This the place where hopes had left
their traces, stark in storm,
stoked in "astonishing nights, foreigners among humans,"
whose eye thirl, window whorl they Open Wide
seeking wordth and depth,
if ever, given
ques and querl, this wordth and depth could be,

who want to speak to sight, to sigh and
rage, *not for that hour, nor for that place*
yet *nowhere*
unembellished by some trace:
documentary (that and more), witnessing (that
many more) and witless, hurtful, "jesting air"—en-
joined, frozen in motion but not to crumble, rather
stand. This has to stand, inside, longside them as
It; and yet is split, is double split, in impulse, turn, and goal.
Still somehow moves (un-
sanctioned? leaden?) fated, stripped,
by road or pathway or through trackless field,
Up hill or down.

What hope then for the wanderer?
Yet and Yet and Yet in place.
Aura of words in a storm face.
There are plenty of reasons to wonder.

Book II

I locked the lightning in my keep, was locked up thus,
smashed by overload, the jagged
space set humming inside shimmered frequency, the treacherous
luminosity, aware that it, or something happened, was this dream
(so when you let the black dog out, brown dog comes back),
of lightning hitting precariously clear, on shadows
of this living willfulness (what to do, where did it go and can you wait
here, now, til other dog comes back? You need the one that was; prattle,
    prattle).
Or is time to leave, thunderstruck, parling, parting the tiny puddle of
    driven?
But then, to hammer in the point, this all came down again—
a blue-white streak of immensity uncontained (sheets of ice;
must walk in spiky heels) a strip of eye, vibrating its cockled
stun, uncanny flash, and same flesh riven
electrically, pink tailed stars of mineral industry with
this exact absolute humming as was, and was, and was inside before.
What about snow? skidded thoroughly, turn left,
I left, but why you turn the other way
you family picnicking in snow as if in summer field, crystal as
"the jesting air of the mountain," up where heads are drooped
dismanaging, as something sounds—the other sides of words that are not
truth or fact or findings fine, but strike as vision strikes—
Nomadic forays in the workshop
of abyss. Here.
Infected with these tremorings of light.
Simply look out, plus then to wake—what is awake?
In certain states of mind this wake cannot console.
The earth was comfortless . . . .
Imploded, a spot irrevocable
    and saturate.

Book III

The Broom so bright (Y as in yellow) corbel flower, lippy sweet, one sudden
day 500 times collapsed upon itself, like tea leaves. Here the checkered Now
sinks sulky plumblines in small places, makes liminal shunts, finds the
odd hole this near. Nearer than here, nearest. Neaten fear. All
(of the above) shuttles back and forth or sinks, steeping.

The future:
(bullet) knotted tendencies
(bullet) visionary horrors
(bullet) coinciding plunder
(bullet) comfortless costs.

"A" figure backlit, note also fig. "B"
the naked wanderer foot misstepped, skidded
 cross *the loose stones that cover the highway*
a falling forward dizzy Fell.
For few have found just covenants that hold.
For here and there are both displayed and crushed.
An immemorable dust
spangled [for those who care at all]
with kindred multitudes of stars
is strewn where we are
where we lie
tense and restless, twisted lot and cowed.
Should we assume there can be real covenant,
not given, not imposed, not crazed, but struggled
for and wide? Or should that hope be
given out as gone?

Book IV

The dawn-y rise of streaks, a puff enormous, silver
edge of rain dropped from the Dictionary of the Pivotal—
this is talking to you? Unknown land, unknown way, along
a plot? a point? "I" "Rainbow" "air time"
wandering phantom of another life.
These words don't count, these rhythms writhe,
this range is wronged, so bye-bye and
depart from? out? beyond?
Words width, wish length, what words worth where
the *discontented sojourner* on *the road's watery*
surface finds Pinhole Specks of light in labyrinthine misery,
for under *the breathless*
wilderness of clouds two Butterflies, black and *bright sprinklings,*
settle matching upside-down to right-side down, their
yellow middle stuff conjoined, and flash a double continuous worm,
being at earnest in a place the wind could not disturb,
and so, *tossing in sunshine* on the narrow stalk, they fucked
and pulsed and this was here, these butterflies and this heated air in which
something created intricacy of its own whirlwind, intimate
vortex of time's heartbreaking precipice.

Book V

Here are the tracks where nomads crossed the surge,
the edge *a bed of glittering light,* inside this unknown land, where
former dwellers now uprooted recognize that they are nomads too.
Tracer arcs of hypnogogic prophecies *in an unknown tongue*
dislodge real outcomes. All struttering ramble
these travelers and survivors, split and mangled,
scrabble over looped and wayward paths, here
at the transition between dream and waking,
in the translation of dream during waking,
in the transliteration of dream's glyphs and icons
into inadequate words upon waking—
Where are we?
what dictionary? what country?
what wake? What tangled
corridors of strangeness?
Dreamed in the dream of telling him the dream.
If half the earth is blown away
will the rest wobble, witless and betrayed?
will it physically shatter or
shit on itself in orbit?

There is the stone
and molten tangles frozen inside stone;
there is the shell
and rainbows of wet nacre
(naccara, from naqqarah: shell).
A shell a stone a book all interfused
a shell plus stone a hardened book
(of stoning) (of shelling)
with distant figments become frage-frage fragments.
I looked for something that I could not find.
The ocean succ . . . dd . . . ee . . . nly pulled back.

The ocean stood and said:
"will disappear,
all black and void.
For It and All will end and be no more."

Then water murmured water will remain.
It was a stalemate, it was erasure and stun, it was the furthest reach
of implacable unknowing in the blind spot
as if an avalanche of acceleration, unstoppable, slid.

Book VI

The stone thrown at a head, like a bird flown in the open room,
rolls quivering into the deepest corners of shadow;
A shell shatters, someone in shock. These are the signs, so
what are the meanings? Interrogated. Criminal
emptying, maximal damage. What does this do?
"If/ then," they say.
If what?
So "Once I interrogated the Muse."
Then I gave up.
After umbra, after aura, after flecks of water-laden light
inside readiness, after *lake, islands,*
promontories, gleaming bays,
breath going in and out of nostrils
fruition of attentiveness,
after densities and extensives,
after the ambient whistle of wandering voices,
after all identification and loneliness,
then two full dreams with frozen legs
destroy the doorway into other dreams.

No walk, dragging lead legs,
legs blown off and blood I see
fated, naked, registers of the squandered
to catch whatever,
the train just left.
I could not find
the half-shaped road which we had missed.

Thought odd in commonness
the dream itself
surprise, how could it be surprise
good bye, she said
(though still alive)
"I am already dead."
And then hung up.
And then go back
and dream it all again
under a long-lived storm.
Botched tracking shot, perjury, complicity,
crime, single crimes amassed.

Not to see hope
is damaging.
To see it, but deluded, could be worse.

Hard to be temperate
yet animated, hard to be ready
yet frozen, hard to think one's whole life's
just gone by,
like placid twists of valley mist past dawn
evaporated, disappeared as if
absolutely nothing had been there.

Book VII

A person with a tattered sign is
freaking out,
that stinking man a shambled sod in rugs
wraptured in the cardboard dirt
rages on the grate: We are FREE-
king out.

need food
need help
need work
need to know
need more
different from this *restless lustre.*
Different from this recklessness.

The socket popped its lumbering bone
the flesh inflamed
the muscle crmpt, the boddy popped
apart, all fall apart,
he breaks the jar, it spilled and smashed,
the soil of self is saturate;
it all ran out upon the ground.
Someone with a message.
This message not to be discussed; it's here.
I stared and listened, with a stranger's ears.
One day was indelible marker on carton,
So that:

Book VIII

Ruthless pious restless precipitate,
solemn conspiracies of certitude;

I have bllod ty3pe
a zero, 0,
number plus or minus oxygen, and a scattered way (a zzz or zig)
of wandering.
Through unregenerate wheat-berry bread
my local clover honey drips.
So if not this, what more?
What then can resist the regime
of human sacrifice?
Fear that we will never be released
fear we will ever
be bound under the whetted knife
following murderous orders
giving murderous commands
being, inside body, those commands.

Book IX

Fair greetings to this shapeless eagerness,
fair greetings to this naiveté, to the whole
exhausting voyage.
Enough of these stories.
Enough, this wandering.

The unbroken dream entangled me.
A drop on the head, a shimmer—
this long unrolling road,
great parchment seamed, on which
I am tumbled down the sluice of the unthinkable
and lie in heap.

Burnt amber. Burnt umber. Burned stone.
Things strewn.
Actually—people smashed into pieces,
speckles of people, pure broken flesh in bits.
Reality too close and too intense.

There is a leak in the house;
the house turned inside out
and all was sucked
down deep unguarded holes.
I dreamed last night I
misneg.   corres-ponge.
Call it an old design
the will of a projection,
call it a statement,
call it out:
in what world I was,
amid the depth
of those enormities.

Book X

The loops of thought and new-mint sound
began to rise along the toil of push.
 Or this was just posturing. It was
 really the small crumple exaggerated
 pinch and poke; poppit, prime and pry.

So *from the rubbish gathered up a stone.*
Then from the rubble gathered up a stone.
One for the heavy-laden grave.
Two for the split in the person.
Three, three,
and on and on.

But then began a rubble wall.
Random pieces placed in counter-poise.

Slate, granite and conglomerate,
sandstone, limestone,
brick, and shale

wedged up from field or quarried from,
or found and piled, or gathered up
along the dusty sides of road.

The force retained as each rock balances.
The brightened chips of brick
get set at angles.

Sometimes such a wall will stand, or
even under pressure
only shatter round the edges

because of bonded energy.
The properties
of various
stones and of mixed
elements
allow for inner motion and for
give and hold.

This is one thought, sometimes proportionate.
Although sometimes not.

Voices of the dead give speeches on these principles of physics.

Book XI

Even the fastidious
drink blood
though it is not presented
exactly as blood
but sweetened, crinkle-packaged,
bright-named something else.

These details are not seen unless enlarged.
Yet the photo was also altered digitally
to remove any buildings and detritus
unwanted in the "scene"
as not seen, nor to be seen,
as neither reality nor not;
it was a new kind of reality
perhaps the river
as it was once in
"history" without that bridge
or billboards fronting up that hill.
Or dream, perhaps a dream. Brown dog come back.
But where was black one left?
To enlarge and to remove were charming acts.
So this was art. But did it make you see?

And betrayed.
Betrayed by plunderers,
betrayed by prophets,
betrayed by law and lawlessness alike,
by false judges and by faked facts,
I lost all feeling of conviction.

The world is aflame!
Sonata form or telos cannot register

the dark clustering of underside
ghettoized here,
ghetto ghetto ghetto. And
there is no pronoun
that is not
agglom.

"Let this time have its canto."
Yes, let it!

Book XII

So it became a question
of someone setting out, and setting forth,
faltering and faint, and ignorant of the road
and then
of checking where one ended up
wherever stumbled feet did fall—at the border
(what border?), at the prelude
(to another Prelude?).
Which are facts? And which are shadows?
Which is the door and which is the wall?
Who was carrying oars? And why?
In another kind of woulds or woods, or weirs
all willful and
yet driven against roots and sluice by turbulence,
entangled in the surge,
the exhilarating mournfulness of time,
the accelerating mournfulness speaks

for the pillaged griot staggering
into *the dark abyss intent to hear.*
"The path we travel . . .
fundamentally just such a ghost walk."

Book XIII

And here are apples again behind the silly wall.
As many kinds as still can grow despite industrial agriculture,
in little pockets of rocky, hard-cleared field,
red and yellow, pocky brown and green
gotten picked by myth yet still growing.
The nature of the frame
no longer taken for granted, and
with these apples, the frame is pippins too.
So the notions of flicker
and edge (as form, as desire, as credibility)
grew in intensity
along a perpetually irregular
line. And so this querying, curious
harvest trips its place in advance, offers imagination
of itself, like a premonitory preparation for
the time in which the traveler is swept upon a flood
of light and pain, a *glittering light*, a circumfusion of pain.
Depressed, bewildered thus
through times of shame
washed up on disturbed ground
tired, without force, impatient with it all,
one can still say A for apple. A for anger.
A for anguish. And/ Or eat an unripe, sour fruit.
At least what is. This being what it is.

Book XIV

I lost neither my anger
though it became a dark stone
smoothed by salty water
nor my sadness
summed up as a collect of bleached-out shells.
And opening a letter
that had been torn in half even before
it was delivered,
"I"
and "leap."

Pilgrimage demanded no less.
Justice demanded no more.
Even the jump, the loss,

the rage. Hand might shatter glass
hand might shatter itself
in bloody glass—

The blood comes thru the book.
A writing made of blood is not
so easily effaced. So
Tumult and peace; since
the darkness and the light
helix and join, and
the historical air clotted here
as luminosity and ruin
must still be breathed and lived
as now, where all this is and are.

JUNE 2005–JANUARY 2007

Draft 75: Doggerel

> Who would succeed, as well as greatly think,
> Must sing by Rule, and ne'er in language sink.
> > John Bancks, "Weaver's Miscellany"

Caffeine curls on the tired tongue,
news in the head. Pull the bung
and in floods bungle, spin and angle,
backwashing sink of political tangle.
Mug of the month, sneeze of the day,
whose germ warfare? Bombs away!
Then re-lost my watch (this, farcical. Again?)
but had no trouble counting minutes, when
New War hopefuls rode their highest horse,
come to kill us, scorch us (trial by fire, of course)
by Mono-Vision "Light." Or lure us and secure us.
It's perils of Pauline (again!) on the road to Tsuris.
History's lined us up against the wall, all of us, and any.
Truly WWIII or IV is one or two too many.

What's a good-enough response to pickles made of quandary?
The Golden Treasury? The aureate maunder-y?
It's dog-trot jogging down this busy road, alert
to those who'll trash you since you "wear a skirt."
Fishing in modernist streams on a feminist page
with lines of enigma held on poles of rage,
I catch the fish once called "détournement,"
a pissed-off, slimy one who swims in *honte*.
It's shame, thick-piled in nook, and mine, and cranny.
Declare a war (or not!), fire up, and gun yer granny.
All in the name of One or Another Holy Irritant—
outrageous claims "*to be the true Church Militant:*
Such as do built their faith upon
The holy text of pike and gun."

When I hear tell of heaven's selfish gravy
I think these faith-based folk are lit'rally crazy.
When I see they foresee their Last Days barbecue ⎫
expecting the damned (secularist, Jew,   ⎬
gay, atheist and more) to roast in meaty queue, ⎭
or believe the State's conversion to their preachers' croon—
well! not voluntarily, not likely, and not soon!
As for mealy, excusing, liberal doublespeak—
Its long-run hit show is "Babbitt Méchanique."

Some who mean *enormous* will say *enormity*.
The same ones know for sure *religiosity*
is a forceful, stronger word that means *religious*.
(Plausible, *that* one, but rather unpropitious.)
Full and *fulsome* are, to those, the same.
I think that women's lib should take the blame
for this and so much more. Like Sexual License.
Female dress *should* be dressage. Stone them into niceness.

Archaic sexist proverbs ego in her head
The ancient hunky wisdom of the dead.
The current denial of female human rights?
Return to the field; we will re-fight those fights.
Still, Dog caught roped around the fence
feels trapped, feels bad, makes noise, wants hence,
the shortest way to home. Bow wow.
O silly dog, the shortest way
              is gone. Can only take the long way now.

That women are dogs is fact quite well known
(to truest Believers re-gnawing that bone):
only of use when they're muzzled or led,
in Evil whenever they're given their head.
Women are dogs, and po'try is what?

Here is an answer; might please you a lot.
The one part of dog that will never be missed
is the first three letters of the word *dogmatist*.
Hence the optimal way to resist rigid "God's Will" ⎫
that, for dreadful bad "Good," has decided to kill, ⎬
is affirming the tolerant Method of Dog-gerel. ⎭

SO: what is poetry, well, swain, what is it?
If you have no standard, how to tell the sh-t
from Shineola ®. Or the real from neither?
In troth, take both, I'm loathe to impose either.
A claim, at risk of imprecating curses:
That *"rhyme the rudder is of verses."*
Those who can, do; who can't, canter,
their cant says doggerel-mode is only banter.
NOT SO!
Contemp'rary poetry too oft sounds self-same.
So what's then wrong with dogg'rel's pelf-claim?
It maximizes poet-acrobatic markers;
insists on slick mouth skills of circus barkers.
I say that doggerel really gets it right, at last.
Up doggerel, wreck refinement, go for crass.
If crude, please analyze why crude is scorned.
Unwieldy? Tell what's hegemonic norm.
If naïve, o simperer, please list for me
up-market decorums that avoid naiveté.
If an easy lay to make, I'd give the lie
to lay, nix easy, and its double sex-
entendre, that desire to hex
the female position. Subject p—for sure.
Lay or lie, such fits have their allure.

This drasty rhyming thing has got me lured. ⎫
More worth than well-prized verse oft-heard. ⎬
Exception: Chaucer's untoward "toord." ⎭
All anti-doggish rumors are designed
as catty cunnings of an under-crafted mind
to clear the way for "better" (theirs)—my worse.
Let's <Vex> our deep-mouthed poetry to verse
with friendly, thousand percent mangled
lines. Make jingle so the reader gets all jangled.
What is "it flows" as well-rewarded praise
compared to how it stumbles, trips, and splays?
Besides This Poetry could earn real money
as star of stage or screen or ads—it's funny.
Who wouldn't want a bit of extra cash
Cooking Amer-Canad-English into hash.
Quirks quick, using "25 words or less." (That's fewer.)
Works us over, red, white and truer-bluer.
"Writing a book? going for glory?
Well, kiss my ass. There's your love story."
Dump poems winning Goodie Two Shoes prizes.
I want dervishing data, disgraceful devices.

Yet what is the meaning of doggerel from dog?
if jumping's the point why not froggerel from frog;
if pinguid engorgement, try hoggerel from hog;
if bumpy and wooden, use log-roll from log.
That canine I lived with had reasons to pout.
He wanted him in when I wanted him out.
He's too strong, too useless, he lies on the couch,
snags napkins and pens; brays, snuffles, bites—Ouch!—
but for all Big-Dog Faults, of rhyme he's not guilty.
His paws may be large and his jowls may drool filthy,
but doggerel's canard upon him and his kin.
A -nomer that's mis-, a –sult of his in-.

Although I suppose that in matters canicular
you can't be too Sirius, or even too particular.
So we're stuck with this word, whether lite-bright or dumb-dumb,
though dictionary defs. cannot tell where it comes from.

I'll defend to the breath not the dog trot or dog cart
but the woman, as best source of poetic dog-art,
form being no more than extensions of cunt-tent,
Best woman, best thought gets the poem unbent.
It's a logic as good as most rampant today
when we make war (not love) or get blown out of the way. ⎫
I say women are dogs and that doggerel's OK. ⎬
Only women are poets, only girls get the bay. Yea! ⎭

Still, this dogged defense of one gender for mammals
doesn't solve the dilemma of Poetic Trammels.
Is doggerel the purest tip-top poem-making, ⎫
gold standard for wince-induced moments of quaking? ⎬
the nice mode for freeze-burn (or freezer-dried) aching? ⎭
Or is doggerel the symptom of poetaster disease,
a tumbling avalanche that wastes paper trees,
a cheap tactic for satirists probing the lax,
the supine conformists, the formalist hacks,
the Skulls sending Your kids, not their own, to fight.
Yell "bad poem" (like "bad dog"), "you're a blight."
Yet prosody handbooks praise "poems" like this. ⎫
My judgment's awry, my panties a-twist— ⎬
wrong-right, dogtrot-epic, pudding or schist. ⎭
All these opposites and binary formations—
Undo them, screw them, lose yr patience.
See? My doggerel's full of didactic elation,
ut this, and *ut* that. *Ut* it all! Here's your ration.

Poets are those knowing how words may mix,
troping the troop so they toot some cute tricks.
Poets specialize in meter and rhyme;
doggerel excels at, accelerates time.
Poem essence, folks say, equals this: rhyme and meter.
And Doggerel produces. It couldn't be neater.
It's proven three times to be poem at its best.
Thrice-repeated illogic puts all doubt to rest.
If these achievement criteria are as absolute
as Religion or War claims, without one single *doute*,
then this is poet's poetry, the poem's poem, poetissima
unleashed, unbounded, optimal bonissima.

Syntax trumps sense, meter rides o'er syntax,
rhyme hits up all with hockey stick wacks,
a punishment come from insisting on worse win
gamely, in Name of (Nom du) Pair Gershwin.
This manner of poem you want to deem "rough"? ⎱
Your laureate's limp. You clearly lack stuff   ⎬
to revise dinky verslets right up to snuff.   ⎰
You tax your readers with metrical monotony.
Reading your work is like instant lobotomy.

So I'll just rattle on with grotesque textuality
straining the leash of your vexed liberality,
pretending a wide-eyed, cute subjectivity,
oblivious to badness—and to my proclivity.
Breath must have death, and thus, satisfaction,
love and above, a knee-jerk reaction.
Do not neglect moon and June with a spoon.
Resist, if you can, sour cream cum raccoon.
Can *you* tell what conventions are best for this time?
Then precisely what's wrong with my rattle-on rhyme?
Who could want to be high-lit'rary merely—

like just being male when we all could be queerly.
Who could want to be bored with correct recipe
when cooking and spicing and stirring is glee.
Doggerel's so bad that it can't come to grief.
It's Two Thousand and Five. We need Comic Relief!
We need more mixage-drivel, less straight-edged bevel.
We need poetry played on the mishegoss level!

Enough already? of going round and coming round. But no—
there's plenty further coming round to go.

DONE VARIOUS TIMES
BETWEEN JUNE 2000 AND JULY 2005

Draft 76: Work Table with Scale Models

1.
5 1/2 × 8 1/2. A sense of loss is pleated, crumpled,
then pressed onto the page,
texturing the bond with shadowy lotteries.
Is it shredding or building; neutral, engaged,
morph and/or decay?

Yes.
The condition of being
under the changeable sun in the,
although smallish to us, vast
and lustrous spaces
of accidental time, lithic
melancholy,
and milky wrinkles
is—what it is.

2.
First,
It and
is red. Red wet crickets slow
down when
the mix of hot and cold is too
much for them.
And green.
Cicada carcasses on the sidewalk,
crisp ashen wings.
Nothing to say. Just
gleaming.

Gleaming!

3.
Here: a pile of cut grass and twigs, naked, dry, a pile that, when
picked up, amazingly sticks together. This random pile *of* stuff, it
holds together! Weedy vectors and cross-hatched shims, the
spaces between, the material unevenness, the math and after-
math, the balance and torque, the splay and force. Only a little
falls off.

4.
In the void
the alphabet clumps, shivers,
and gathers in,
rolling itself
in front of itself.

5.

[Nothing to build.
DUNKEL as model.
This gap not "filled."
It is finally (almost) literal.]

6
occurs as mixed doubles:
scumbling and glazing,
tarring and tattering,
overleaf and blockage.

But the relation of one to the other, and their interplay
color to undercoat, transparent to opaque, mist to glimpse?

Twinned alternatives
loop and lurch
between precarious contradictions
and precipitate affirmations.

7.

    Bright lamps only manage this despair.
        Therefore turn
        off the light!
    Look into the dark news.

Its Place-markers are shadow traces.
Its Medicant Envoys
presenting themselves and their credentials
get ploughed like letters into the palimpsest.

    I knew what I wanted. It was darkness
        endlessly overwritten
        (dark-news, I listen);
    I wanted a "swirling mutedness," although in words.

8

registers no telling what.
    Motif of shadow,
        Motif of whisper,
Hard to point to.
    The Wedge-shaped Ricochet
        over the swathe.
The *the* and
-the.

Record these
without
tampering with

this.

9.
Found paper & thread
piths and plis
a pile of folded quires
hid in the abandoned pavilion of verses,

found paper & thread
undid the book
low hum and rustle, voiceless
out of the fallen leaves of text.

Re-bound the folds with sweet reeds and whiplash

tied polylingual billets, doux ding-a-ling,

And punched andare-ritornare

tickets, there and back,

one for entering the book

one for escaping the book.

10.
Say "epistle." Then "stel-." The proto-Indo-European appendix of
my *American Heritage Dictionary* gives to put, stand, set object,
send or place. Gives quiet, fixed, still; apostle, diastole, peristalsis,
put in order, prepare; gives standing place: stable, pedestal, or

gestalt; gives stallion, stale and stall; gives branch or shoot, stolon and stolid, stalk, stilt and stick; strut and stout. And stele. These induce pungent forays into shreds of unconnected narrative, core-cuts into social and psychological strata, plus the jerky vectors of uneven suggestiveness. Precisely the gift. Sensations multiply, and no one can put them all "into" words. Although they are words. And *words* is where they come from. This exists and under-mines; it affirms and negates. For you are a collect of their socio-twisty selves; you are a splinter of their sharded conditions. Yet you are their rhetor. This is not passivity and binding, but plea-sure and entitlement from the loss of much—but not all—adjudi-cating will, as the pulse of language tries its visceral routes through your own engorgement and resistance. Language with its ferocious, elegant flood of desire and demands is rising toward you, through you, while you are startlingly enraptured just at the point of coming, to at least partial understanding.

11.
Descant, to thread thru rant
          a wire. Cannot hear them, what we are marked by
          Cannot see the *the* we are marked by
          Cannot touch them, that we are marked by.
Know them only
inside this futurial netting.
White noise
(still speaks)
words blacked out
 (still speak)
It
(still
speaking)
is still, speaking.
Language

wishes to be spoken.
It's just its listeners
are bereft.

12.
I had wanted to write just small, though hungry, sentences,
small.
But so much wells up at once it is like
externalizing a gigantic wall.

13.
The talismans of this or that are handed round.
Their "folds come to contain the flow of time."
Fold to flow, come to con-, tain to time.
Beautiful.   Really.
And this is also a theory of debris.
Not ironic, but saturated in irony.

14
is missing.
One of those lost things.
Have no sense of where it got to.
Maybe misplaced into another folder,
misnamed, misfiled, miscast,
an accident, that coiled machine,
its malicious caprice, its twittering
in the face of—tragedy.
There's nothing (therefore)
(so to speak) in this spot.

15.

Can't have it too empty. Can't have it too full. Aware
        in any event, of jumpiness and then settling.
        At least a cryptic outline:

shadow words slouching shadow-wards;
images rich in the intensive;
bird call knots and frilly tn-nhh trills;
flowers in the feathery grass, grainy, peppering;
items in a series shot through with the inexplicable . . .

and so on.

16.

"A little epic" but hardly
vivid or learnèd; digressive
but never gets anywhere specially, but here.

All sublime and insistent moments, quick send-ups inter-cut
all realist wandering
diagonal
saturated
exceeding itself
if it's really lucky
picking along the narrow space
in the pressure zone
between y and n.

17.

Is it just about line, form, intention, drip, bands?
Is it just about drape, conceptual comment,
the rupture of assumptions one way or the other?
Axle? Axis? Ekstasis? Indifference?
Chance, luck, loss, contempt,
is it just about illusion, allusion, citation, repetition?

All of it,
friction, template, almanac,
all about every word,
minute-by-minute
responsibility
mise à nu,
discretionary of slang,
rife numerology and intensification of snap.

It is always involved and involuted,
not at the center of
the day, but always
Uneven, always Odd,
always
Off.

18.

Painstakingly to translate once Anglophone words from French or
Italian back into English, or from English to English, or from
anything to anything else, watching them shimmer, modulate,
differ. Or accidentally to find writing—who did that? Words
arranged so, from the damage of days in the general seeking and
shattering. These words remind a person intermittently that
something had occurred and is still occurring, and this happens
over and over, so that the whole, someone might say, is one poem
articulated a hundred-odd ways, yet, at the same time, the whole
is so many different works that it cannot be unified or accounted
for. This could be called a failure. I mean, a pleasure.
(Precisely to have failure—on that scale and with that level
of stubbornness—was one of the few things I foresaw.)

19.
Clear the table! Break this allegiance!
Scatter the little machines!
Begin!
Here! And Here!

But could be screen works parlaying pixilated fields.
And could be screen words.
Or a few selected words with shadowy opera behind them—?

$$\text{wor} < \begin{matrix} \mathbf{D} \\ \\ \mathbf{K} \end{matrix}$$

in a No No No

tebook

"My works get made and then chopped up, and then reglued and remade, and then chopped up again, the whole thing is really endless."

July–September 2005

Notes

Notes to Draft 58: In Situ. On March 20, 2003, a student named Kishan Sheth jumped to his death from Anderson Hall, Temple University. The "istrici" are, *inter alia*, an allusion to Jacques Derrida, "Che cos'è la poesia," in which poetry gets compared to hedgehogs, hérissons, or istrici. In Umbria, what we know as porcupines in the U.S. are also called istrici. This is the first poem of the fourth group of 19.

Notes to Draft 59: Flash Back. This draft was very loosely inspired in the aftermath of a chain work initiated by Dodie Bellamy for the Buffalo Poetics List in 2000. I participated with an untitled statement that proposed the instability of gender and sexuality in dreams and then offered a homophonic translation of this thought, thus creating a kind of "chora" or babble that matched and doubled the analytic proposal. The respondent to this was Brian Kim Stefans, who constructed a work called "The Dream Life of Letters" by alphabetizing the words in my statement, arranging them in mini-sections, and, using a Flash program, made, with wit and visual acumen, an animated text and a web poem from the words and letters, certainly transforming the text I wrote. The result, in his words, was a "long flash animation poem with a twist of avant-feminist lime." URL access *http://www.ubuweb*. In the poem "Not to oedipalized, Duh to enterprise, Me to non" are from Stefans' index of the units of his work. In an e-mail interview from March 2001, Stefans also briefly discussed this set of tactics with Darren Wershler-Henry. Wershler-Henry asked whether the transformational tactics of this work did not compromise the feminist speculation in my statement. See Stefans, *Fashionable Noise: On Digital Poetics* (Atelos, 2003). The "wanderful": Marisa Berna. "Vigorous scribbles" suggesting "deep space" is from the Jasper Johns show, February 1999, Philadelphia Museum of Art. *Fruta da época* simply means fruit of the season in Portuguese, but the false friend *epoch* was interesting to me. Later in the poem, *Furia azul* (Blue Rage) is the name of a contemporary Portuguese anarchist group whose graffiti I saw in 2003. *Niente da vedere, niente da nascondere* means nothing to see, nothing to hide; it is a motto of Alighiero Boetti, from the Italian Arte Povera movement. The last line is an almost-accurate citation from Bonnie Costello, "Planets on Tables: Still Life and War in the Poetry of Wallace Stevens." *Modernism/Modernity* 12. 3 (Sept. 2005), 451. Donor drafts are the whole "line of 2": She, Cardinals, and One Lyric.

Notes to Draft 60: Rebus. Rainer Maria Rilke's *Duino Elegies* (1922), especially certain lines, have long haunted me. Taking (on) some version of his lines and phrases and some of his situations finally became inevitable. I have underscored the citations, mainly using the A. Poulin, Jr. translation, sometimes with slight modifications. In his Preface to the Houghton Mifflin book (1977), Poulin says "I hope someone else will find a word or phrase to steal from these versions." He meant other translators, of course, but I thank him for his generosity in any case. The epigraph from Martin Heidegger, Epilogue, "The Origin of the Work of Art." Donor Drafts are on the "line of 3": Of, Philadelphia Wireman, and Of This.

Notes to Draft 61: Pyx. Ezra Pound has been an essential modernist for Anglo-American poetry, and among the practitioners haunted by his work and his career, I would count myself. The bold-face citations from Ezra Pound come from *Canti postumi*, a significant selection of outtakes and draft versions of Pound's *Cantos*, edited by Massimo Bacigalupo, Milan: Mondadori, 2002, a facing page edition of the English with Italian translations, along with some Canto materials written in Italian. These citations are, respectively "My mind stretched to the bursting point . . . the gun-sales," 204, from 1945. "Ledt hoo vill rhun de harmies . . . gredit," 102, from 1928–37. "Greasy flame of dead gas flare" and "a thick air," 104, also from 1928–37. "Some narrow rat . . . on Mt. Arrarat" [sic], 232, from 1949–60. "How is it? I said: that the ghosts are so gathered?" 160, from 1940–45, and "ombra sono e ombra fui" [shadow I am and shadow I was], 175, from 1944–45. Other citations are as follows: Epigraph by Barrett Watten, *Total Syntax*, Carbondale: Southern Illinois U.P., 1985, 102. "The melodic germ is marked 'icy' in the score" from program notes by John Corigliano for his "Etude Fantasy," 1976. The material about the deported is my riff on Jerome Rothenberg's words in conversation. "The stench of stale oranges" is from Pound, Canto XIV, one of the "Hell Cantos." "I sat to keep off the impetuous, impotent dead" is from Pound, Canto I. I am grateful to the poet Anne Blonstein for email discussions of a provisional, unused title to this poem. Donor Drafts along the "line of four": In, Findings, and Epistle, Studios.

Notes to Draft 62: Gap. In 1986, Jochen Gerz and Esther Shalev-Gerz made a counter-monument "Against Fascism, War, and Violence—and for Peace and Human Rights" set in Harburg (a suburb of Hamburg, Germany). Counter, because it is no longer "there." It was a 12-meter / 40 foot high lead-covered column of aluminum with steel-tipped styluses attached. After each 5-foot section was covered with statements, scrawls and graffiti, it was lowered into a prepared chamber. This monument, created precisely to disappear from view, was begun in 1986; it disappeared totally into its site in 1993. This poem draws on information in James E. Young, *At Memory's Edge: After-Images of the Holocaust in Contemporary Art and Architecture*, Yale U.P., 2000; it is not a direct commentary on this memorial. "It is proper to go back to the shadows," cited from Luce Irigaray. The poem is, like Draft 31: Serving Writ, deliberately short. Donor drafts are the Drafts also called Gap.

Notes to Draft 63: Dialogue of self and soul. There are a few citations from W.B. Yeats' "A Dialogue of Self and Soul" and "Ego Dominus Tuus." The Biblical allusion (one of the patterns of the "line of six") is 1 Samuel 4.

Notes to Draft 64: Forward Slash. The famous ditch is modified from Filippo Marinetti, "Futurist Manifesto." The citation is from Jane Caplan.

Notes to Draft 65: That. The two translators of Bashō's title are Cid Corman and Sam Hamill. The final line comes from Theodor Adorno, *Prisms*, citing Arnold Schönberg, 164. This poem was written after the death of William Van Wert.

Notes to Draft 66: Scroll. "For each person in the world to reach present U.S. levels of consumption with existing technology would require four more planet Earths." E.O. Wilson, *The Future of Life*. Dumping in the field is a reminiscence of the 2001 Agnes Varda film called (in English) *The Gleaners and I*. "Trigger Treat" is something kids may say on Hallowe'en, a fact noticed by Lorine Niedecker. "Every poem has an alter ego," Jed Rasula, *This Compost: Ecological Imperatives in American Poetry*, Athens: University of Georgia Press, 2002, 79. The incident in stanza two is based on work by Shostakovich, the String Quartet number 8 in C minor, opus 110, and it was said about Shostakovich himself (notes for the CD of the Borodin String Quartet's recording); this quartet is dedicated "to victims of fascism and war." The end of stanza two is a modified version of the end of *Un Coup de Dés*: "veillant/ doutant/ roulant/ brillant et méditant." In the Daisy Aldan translation: "Watching/ doubting/ revolving/ blazing and meditating"; in the J.P. Houston translation: "keeping vigil/ in doubt/ turning/ luminous and meditative"; in the translation by Henry Weinfield: "keeping vigil/ doubting/ rolling/ shining and meditating." *In tempore belli* (in time of war) used by George Crumb to date his string quartet "Black Angels" (1970). "Materials have memory" stated by Alison Saar about her collages: "I love the idea that materials have memory, the idea of working with materials that have experienced more than I have." Saar in an interview with bell hooks, in *Art on My Mind*, 22. "There are no sentences performed without residue," was said once in class by Melody Holmes. "Dimensions that are tightly curled into the folded fabric of [the cosmos]" from Brian Greene, *The Elegant Universe: Superstrings, Hidden Dimensions, and the Quest for the Ultimate Theory*, 6. Donor drafts along the "line of nine": Page, Facing Pages, and Printed Matter.

Notes to Draft 67: Spirit Ditties. Section 1. Social surrealism, e.g. the work of Walter Quirt seen at the Hartford Atheneum. The citation closing the same section is from artist Valerie Hollister. Section 12. Bird song citations from Harry Gilonis, *Learning the Warblers*, especially "chakakakaka," "churr, tcharr, chairr," "zi-CHEH zi-CHEH" and "gee-yip-ee." With thanks to Peter and Meredith Quartermain. Section 16. Techne of weaving from sheep to cloth, courtesy of Robert DuPlessis. Shepherd to poet information—Hesiod, *Theogony*. Section 20. Abuse from the bridge and the wagon, Elusinian mystery processions in ancient Greece. Section 21. The line about the ransacking of cemeteries is taken from English explanations in the Etruscan Museum at Chiusi. Section 22. "Images say, 'Behold!'" Adorno, *Aesthetic Theory*, 168. Another serial poem, along the "line of ten."

Notes to Draft 68: Threshold. "Boiling gurge of pulse" from Keats, *Hyperion*, Book II. The lines "The room moves into the doorway /which makes the room smaller" are from "The War Years," a serial poem I wrote in c. 1965–67. The gloss language started with some comments made by Michael Davidson at a conference. "There are no words for this, and these are them" (out of John Cage): Charles Bernstein, "today's not opposite day," *With Strings*. The donor drafts are Schwa, Fosse, and Turns (11, XXX, 49). "It can happen that the [literary] work is not written *for someone*, but to dismantle the complex mechanism of frustration and the infinite forms of oppression." Edouard Glissant, *Caribbean Discourse*, 107.

Notes to Draft 69: Sentences. In his introduction to his translation of Paul Celan's *Breathturn* (*Atemwende*), Pierre Joris cites Celan's 1960 Meridian speech which contains the phrase "eine radikale In-Frage-Stellung der Kunst," translated by Gerhard Buhr as a "radical putting-into-question of art." (Introduction, Sun & Moon Press, 20). In Czeslaw Milosz's *A Treatise on Poetry*, one of his lines about the pre-fascist moment is: "When the letter falls out of the book of laws" (translated by Robert Hass; The Ecco Press/ HarperCollins, 2001, p. 29)."The behest of reality": Sigmund Freud, "Mourning and Melancholia," from 1915. The donor drafts are Diasporas, Serving Writ, and Scholia and Restlessness (12, 31, and L).

Notes to Draft LXX: Lexicon draws for its two-and-more-than-two/thirds alphabets on the number of drafts to date, drawing letters and words, in order, from each numbered poem. Thus in Draft 1, I looked for words beginning with the letter A, in Draft 2, I looked for words beginning with the letter B, and so on, and I used some of those words as my palette, arriving at R as the final letter of this poem. That this tactic got amusingly complicated should come as no surprise. "Will no one tell me what she sings?" is from Wordsworth's "The Solitary Reaper." Poesia para/ poesia pura: These terms are from Haroldo de Campos, and mean, respectively "poetry of commitment, poetry for something" and "pure poetry." De Campos puns on Mallarmé: "un sens plus POUR aux mots de la tribu." (In Jerome Rothenberg and Pierre Joris, eds. *Poems for the Millennium*, volume 2, Berkeley: University of California Press, 1998, 315). The word "potrebbero" is Italian for a present conditional: they might. The donor drafts are Haibun, Renga, and Clay Songs (13, 32, and 51).

Notes to Draft 71: Headlines, with Spoils. "**Auto and plant emissions linked to fetal harm**" *The Philadelphia Inquirer*, Feb. 16, 2005, A12. "All of this has been reviewed and is legal. However, I am sorry that there are perceptions and allegations of ethical lapses." Stated by then U.S. Education Secretary Rod Paige. By-line Ben Fuller, *The Philadelphia Inquirer* Jan 14, 2005, A6. Headline was "**Education Dept. to probe payment; senators seek files.**" "Trick in the full *tricked* sense of the word" is a direct citation of Rodrigo Toscano's differently punctuated lines "<trick> <in the full *tricked*> <sense of the word>" from his "State and Sensibility," *The Poker* #6, p. 20. "12 hours per day for a pittance, living 12 to a room, working in fenced-in factory complexes." By-line Erik Eckholm, *International Herald Tribune*, Aug 23, 2001, p. 4; headline was "**China's Workers Lose Protection.**""**Shopping binge compensates for a low industrial sector.**" *International Herald Tribune* , Aug.

24, 2001. [The prototype military robot] "readied, aimed and fired at a Pepsi can, performing the basic tasks of hunting and killing." By-line Tim Weiner, *New York Times*, Feb 16, 2005, C1, C4. Headline was "**A New Model Army Soldier Rolls Closer to the Battlefield.**" Pepsi®. "**Tanker Sinks off Spain, threatening eco-disaster. (Worst spill since Valdez is feared).**" By-line Seth Borenstein and Daniel Rubin; *The Philadelphia Inquirer*, A1. About the tanker Prestige, November 19 or 20, 2002. Headline: "A Cruel Past Lingers (Echoes of the Killing fields. Cambodians in Philadelphia are still haunted, years later and a world away. First of three parts)." By-line Adam Fifield. *The Philadelphia Inquirer*, December 12, 2004, A1. "Smart dust" is "a term to describe communicating sensors no bigger than grains of sand that might be strewn by the thousands on fields and forests. Smart-dust proponents envision such sensors being used to monitor forests for fire, warn soldiers of dangerous substances on the battlefield and alert border guards to activity in remote areas." By-line Barnaby J. Feder. *International Herald Tribune*, July 26, 2004, p. 9. Headline was "**Sensors give a feel to technology.**" In the poem, this citation was somewhat modified. Donor Drafts are Conjunctions, Deixis, Midrash (14, 33, 52).

Notes to Draft 72: Nanifesto. Actually what Kurt Schwitters did make, in his 1922 "Cow Manifesto," were suggestions about arranging things so that every person "can drink from the udder of his personal cow" (Schwitters, in Mary Ann Caws, ed. *Manifesto: A Century of Isms*. Lincoln: University of Nebraska Press, 2001, 390). "You must talk with two tongues": Wyndham Lewis, "Vortex No. 1, Art Vortex." *Blast #2* (July 1915), 91 (facsimile reprinted by Black Sparrow Press, 1981). Although he had been commissioned to write a string quartet, "The work seemed to acquire a will of its own," Einojuhani Rautavaara said, about his 1997 string quintet "Unknown Heavens"; "it wanted two cellos, clearly demanding a second cello." From notes for a CD produced by Ondine Inc, Helsinki. The artist Giacomo Balla did in fact design Futurist golf sweaters. Donor drafts are Little, Recto, Eclogue (15, 34, 53).

Notes to Draft 73: Vertigo. Not to implicate others, but the following people helped with their versions of Mallarmé's work: Henry Weinfield, with his committed translations and discussions in *Stéphane Mallarmé, Collected Poems* (Berkeley: University of California Press, 1994), Charles Bernstein, with the homophonic "Salute" in *My Way* (Chicago: University of Chicago Press, 2001), and Serge Gavronsky with *Mallarmé Spectral ou Zukofsky au Travail* (Limousin: La Main Courante, 1998), a study that located Zukofsky's pun on "oe" ("A"-19, 423). Citations, near-citations, recalibrations and homophonic irruptions draw on "Eventail" and "Un Coup de Dés." I have also at various times been indebted to Daisy Alden's and Anthony Hartley's translations of, and Leo Bersani's version of, Mallarmé. The child-written letters, saved up for many years, courtesy of Koré DuPlessis. The word "dado" means die or cube in Italian, and, as poet John Tranter pointed out, also means the lower portion of the wall of a room, decorated (as with panels) differently from the upper portion. Aside from a citation from Keats, and allusions to other French poets, "recalculated at a new sampling rate" is the original of my line, from notes to a CD by Charles Wuorinen. Donor drafts are Title, Verso, and Tilde (16, 35, and 54).

Notes to Draft 74: Wanderer. Friedrich Hölderlin actually wrote "The astonishing night, the foreigner among humans" (in "Bread and Wine"), 36; "the jesting air of the mountain" is also Hölderlin, in "Homecoming," 41; the translation is by David Constantine, Friedrich Hölderlin, *Selected Poems*, Bloodaxe Books, 1996. "Once I interrogated the Muse"— "Una volta ho interrogato la Musa"—is Andrea Zanzotto's version of Hölderlin's line "Einst hab ich die Muse gefragt, und sie . . ." (the opening line of his poem of the same name) in Zanzotto's "L'elegia in petèl" ("The Elegy in Petèl" [dialect babytalk]), as translated by Ruth Feldman and Brian Swann, *Selected Poetry of Andrea Zanzotto*, Princeton: Princeton University Press, 1975, 245. Digitally altered photo by Andreas Gursky seen at MoMA in 2001. The citation "Let this time have its canto," from Robert Duncan, "Structure of Rime XVIII," *Roots and Branches*, 67. The changed citation from Walter Benjamin L2, 7, *Arcades Project* is really: "The path we travel through arcades is fundamentally just such a ghost walk, on which doors give way and walls yield."

"I, too, have been a wanderer," from William Wordsworth, *The Prelude* (1805) 6, 252 is like the hidden epigraph of this poem. All italicized citations come from William Wordsworth, *The Prelude*, in *Selected Poetry*, ed. Mark Van Doren, Modern Library, NY: Random House, 1950, given below as book and line number in the order of my poem. In addition, there are allusions to situations in *The Prelude*, Books 5 and 7. The Wordsworth citations are: "not for that hour, nor for that place" (3, 81–82); "nowhere unembellished by some trace" (3, 108); "by road or pathway or through trackless field,/ Up hill or down" (1, 27–29); "The earth was comfortless . . ." (2, 121); "the loose stones that cover the highway" (3, 128); "spangled with kindred multitudes of stars" (3, 162); "discontented sojourner" (1, 8); "the road's watery surface" (4, 380); "the breathless wilderness of clouds" (6, 716); "bright sprinkling" (10, 484) "tossing in sunshine" (7, 45); "a bed of glittering light" (5, 129); "in an unknown tongue" (5, 93); "I looked for something that I could not find" (9, 72); "all black and void" (5, 72); "lake, islands, promontories, gleaming bays" (4, 8); "the half-shaped road which we had missed" (6, 620); "under a long-lived storm" (11, 374); "restless lustre" (8, 412); "I stared and listened, with a stranger's ears" (9, 57); "Fair greetings to this shapeless eagerness" (9, 19); "The unbroken dream entangled me" (10, 410); "Reality too close and too intense" (11, 58); "in what world I was" (10, 64); "amid the depth/ of those enormities" (10, 374–75); "from the rubbish gathered up a stone" (9, 69); "I lost all feeling of conviction" (11, 302-03); "faltering and faint, and ignorant of the road" (12, 247); "[over] the dark abyss intent to hear" (14, 72); "glittering light" (5, 130); "depressed, bewildered thus" (11, 321); "through times of shame" (11, 371); "Tumult and peace, the darkness and the light" (6, 635).

Donor Drafts to 74: Wanderer are Unnamed, Cento, Quiptych (17, 36, 55).

Notes to Draft 75: Doggerel. The epigraph is by the "Weaver" poet of the eighteenth century, John Bancks. There are two citations from Samuel Butler's *Hudibras*. The one about the "Church Militant" is from Part I, Canto I, ll. 194–96, and the one about "rhyme" is from Part I, Canto I, l. 464. The concept of the "New War" is from an essay by Erica Hunt. The Yiddish words: tsuris means trouble; mishegoss means craziness.

Notes to Draft 76: Work Table with Scale Models. The citation in section 13, their "folds come to contain the flow of time," is from Charles Altieri, "Taking Lyrics Literally," *NLH* 32.1 (Winter 2001), 273. The citation that closes section 19 comes from the visual artist Ray Johnson. *Ray Johnson: Correspondences*, ed. Donna De Salvo and Catherine Gudis. Columbus, Ohio: Wexner Center for the Arts and Paris: Flammarion, 1999, 191.

Printed in the United States
89259LV00002B/121-159/A

9 781844 713349